A Certain Life

A Certain Life

Contemporary Meditations
on the Way of Christ

Herbert O'Driscoll

The Anglican Book Centre
Toronto, Canada

1980
The Anglican Book Centre
600 Jarvis Street
Toronto, Ontario
Canada M4Y 2J6

O'Driscoll, Herbert.
A Certain Life
1. Jesus Christ — Meditations. 2. Meditations
I. Title.
BT306.4.035   232   79 – 27010
ISBN 0-919030-50-5
Printed in Canada

*For Arthur Butler,
Bishop and Friend*

Contents

"Where shall I seek thee?" asked my soul of God.
　"Where may I find thee whom I love so much?"
"Seek in the hidden place, in ground well trod.
　There shall I walk with thee, there shall we touch."

"Where is thy body?" asked my soul of God.
　"Where is thy body that it meld with mine?"
"Seek in the holy place my flesh, my blood.
　Both will inhabit thee in bread and wine."

"Where is thy glory?" asked my soul of God.
　"Where is the kingdom for which all hearts long?"
"Seek in the simple place, a manger rude.
　Bow down in wonder at the angels' song."

"Were I to pay thee," said my soul to God,
　"All that I have would be so poor in kind."
"Silver and shining gold are less than wood.
　All that I ask," said God, "is heart and mind."

Preface

In the southern valley of the Jordan River, during the reign of Tiberius Caesar, there developed another among the many local religious movements which seemed to grow out of the very rock and sand itself. The focus of this new movement was a man who had gone into the desert impelled by a fellowship and a solemn vow. Born in Judea, the son of a priest, his name was John. Because he had chosen the age-old symbol of ritual washing, to declare a break with the decadent past and a commitment to the imminent acting of God in history, he was called the "Baptizer."

Thirty years before, when John was still lying in the womb of his mother Elizabeth, a special meeting had occurred. Elizabeth had welcomed her kinswoman Mary on a visit from Galilee, and their meeting had been ecstatic with the expectancy of new life. They had parted, each to her own home. Their sons had grown up in the sharply different environments of Judea and Galilee. One had encountered a religious world polarized between a strong and entrenched institutionalism pitted against radical and intense grass roots movements. The other had experienced the loveliness of the Galileen countryside with its corresponding openness and gentleness of spirit.

The two men met on the bank of the Jordan somewhere near the spot where the river enters the Dead Sea. Around them gathered a cosmopolitan crowd, attracted to this arid, sunken valley by a mixture of curiosity, anxiety, and hope. Jesus had come south from Nazareth, drawn by John's message, yet seeing something beyond it. With his hand in that of John he entered the warm brown water...

Thus began a period of approximately three years which changed all subsequent history. For Christians these are sacred years. They are recorded in the gospel, a mode of writing formed and executed expressly to proclaim this sacredness. These writings are both more and less than history, more and less than biography. For Christians they are not only to be read as past event, but also to be experienced in the present life. As with a play the believer must be more than observer, he or she must become the stage upon which the play is acted out.

My hope and intention in writing these chapters has been to

help others experience the remembered past as the experienced present. I write as a believer for believers. That does not mean that I write from a serene certainty for those who may share that scarce commodity in our troubled age. There is much about which I am uncertain. But of Jesus I am certain. That he lived, formed his community, spoke of a kingdom and died for it, that the community which he formed goes on being eternally renewed — of all this I am certain, for I share its life and draw grace and inspiration from it. Likewise I am certain that he is risen, for I see him in the same goodly company that lives in every place and shows in several ways his love and joy and peace.

For the last, I am certain that he comes as Lord, not merely at a near or distant moment of time, but in the present moment, in the terrifying truths and turmoil of a new humanity being formed from a world old and tired, and in the widespread awareness of his presence in human experience within and beyond the Christian community.

> Christ has died.
> Christ is risen.
> Christ will come again.

Our Lord

*Jesus said, "I shall draw all men to myself,
when I am lifted up from the earth."*

The Christian faith is based on an event anchored firmly in time. It is not a legend, although some of the world's most beautiful legends have clustered around it. It is not a myth, although it possesses great mythological power. It is not a piece of art, although artistic genius has drawn great inspiration from it. It is all these things; yet it is more — it is an event.

Into a world like ours, at a time very like our own, there came a man of such integrity and wholeness, such depth and beauty of personhood, that those who associated with him learned to believe certain things about him. Those beliefs and attitudes did not spring into existence fully formed. They grew as anything alive and organic must grow. They began, like all relationships, with an inarticulated attraction, and often led to sudden exclamations of spontaneous faith. In Caesarea Philippi, in response to Jesus' question, Peter bursts out, "You are the Messiah!" After the resurrection Thomas cries, "My Lord and my God!" The unknown pair who rush breathless from Emmaus speak of their hearts burning within them when they recognize the stranger in the breaking of the bread.

Only in later years are the layers of personal and communal experiences unravelled and articulated. This is done by the writers, among them John and Paul. The innocence and spontaneity of the long ago lakeside is lifted into the majesty of the first chapter of John's gospel.

> When all things began, the Word already was.
> The Word dwelt with God,
> and what God was, the Word was....
> All that came to be was alive with his life,
> and that life was the light of men....
> So the Word became flesh;
> he came to dwell among us, and we saw his glory,
> such glory as befits the Father's only Son,
> full of grace and truth (John 1:1).

This man walked among the people and institutions of his time, and his passing was like a light. This light revealed people in their fragility and pretence and lostness. At the same time it filled them with a longing for the kingdom for which all men and women long, and it communicated to those who came under his influence the certainty that they were loved and affirmed, to a depth which they had never thought possible. His light and his words penetrated the institutional structures which became unaccustomed allies in his destruction. For he exposed the network of ambiguous values, political expediency, and vicious self-interest which are part of all human experience.

We tend as humans to back away from bright lights whether they are actual or metaphorical. We are wary of those who we feel can see through us for what we are. And impersonal structures are apt to deal summarily with people who criticize them or threaten their existence. This is very true of organizations which wield great power. To keep that power they are capable of doing very ugly things. One extremely strong institution, wielding great political and economic power, was prepared to see that Jesus of Nazareth was destroyed in the most brutal and humiliating way that could be devised at the time. His death was so appalling in its cynicism and injustice that it shattered and demoralized the community which had formed around him, and which had identified with his words, his life, and his person. The day after he died that community existed only in the most fragile and pathetic way.

The evidence for what happened next lies with that community. They have left a clear and convincing record of how they became aware that the man they had seen die on the cross was among them in a way which, although it was mysterious and awe-inspiring, left no doubt that his presence and his life and communication was electrifyingly real. That fact of the presence of Jesus with his community, both before and after his resurrection, is the central hope and heart of Christian faith.

The Angel

The angel went in and said to her,
"Greetings, most favoured one! The Lord is with you."

John 1:28

Life begins when a human being says, "Yes." Physically this is true when a man and a woman say, "Yes," to each other. Spiritually it is true when we say, "Yes," to the reality we call God.

The gospel begins in the same way. God probes into the human situation, searching on the wings of his love and his ceaseless urge to create new worlds of being. He probes and searches to find the point of human response. To express the mystery of that probing, the message that is always trying to break into our consciousness, we humans have been given the magnificent concept of angels. We receive this concept at birth, and possess it clearly and vividly in childhood. A loving imagination or even the halting words of an adult can ignite the vision of angels in us, and we fall asleep with the knowledge of a presence and the beating of wings.

In youth we learn to banish our angels, but with divine irony they hover about us in many disguises. In falling in love, in moments of intense living, in almost painful discoveries of great beauty in nature, in relationships, in art, in moments of Presence to which we feel called to respond even though we cannot name them — in all this mosaic of growing to adulthood, we walk and sleep and lie dreaming, or dance or converse, under the shadow of angels' wings. "Turn but a stone," sang Francis Thompson, "and start a wing."

The angel came to a small town, but the town did not notice because it was not the object of the visit. God does not send announcements to towns or parliaments or institutions. God communicates with people, usually one person. Like a surgeon who concentrates the intense radiation of a lasar beam to centre on an infinitesimal bundle of cells in the body, God moves from the infinity of his being and impinges on our finitude, entering the microscopic universe of our individual existence.

The angel addressed her. Here, as always, God takes the initiative. Mary is "troubled." This presence is always troubling,

— this voice, this reality within yet beyond us. When it speaks it urges us to go beyond where we are. It has news of journeys to be taken, changes to be made, demands to be met, tasks to be carried out, growing to be done. We are troubled because this call to new creation is risky. To the girl the angel spoke of conception and pregnancy and a new life. And ever since, every angel sent beating its way across the worlds to a human soul has brought the same challenge and responsibility.

Each of us carries in us the new life which God wishes to be born into the world. The new life which comes into the world is not a memory, enshrined in a distant geography or an ancient history. It is not announced by an angel who alights in our mind on the wings of Elizabethan English, acceptable only because we place the moment in a stained glass world of long ago. This new life is announced urgently in every present moment of our being and in countless different disguises. We sense it in the ringing of a telephone, in a conversation over coffee, in the third verse of a hymn, on a rock by the ocean, at the edge of a prairie highway, in a silence shared with another human being, in a book being read. In all these things, and in many more, we ''entertain angels unawares.''

Mary said, ''Yes,'' And it is supremely important, that we say, ''Yes,'' to the divine probe, ''Yes,'' to the angel who is always hovering. And in our saying, ''Yes,'' we become, as Mary realized she had become, ''the Lord's servant.'' In our saying, ''Yes,'' our souls begin to magnify the Lord, and our spirits rejoice in God our Saviour.

The Inn

A decree was issued by the Emperor Augustus . . .
so Joseph went up ... to register at... Bethlehem...
with him went Mary who was betrothed to him.
She was expecting a child.

Luke 2:1

Augustus Caesar and Jesus of Nazareth form a fascinating duality. Both are seen at different times by millions as "Son of God." Both are looked to as "prince of peace." Yet each possesses a kind of power totally different from the other. One possesses legions, the other disciples. One issues a command to conquer, the other a command to love. For a moment these two lives impinge on one another, one of them on the throne of the world in Rome, the other alive in Mary's womb in Nazareth. Without knowing it Augustus sends the holy one on a journey that is to end at the world's end.

This journey could not have been other than inconvenient. We forget that it could have proved fatal. Those miles are demanding miles, some of them through raw, dangerous country. Yet the seed in the womb is asked to survive this, just as in our lives, a newly conceived resolution, a recently discovered friendship, or a special responsibility is tested at the very beginning. Often the seed of a newly found faith is tried in the plain and everyday reality of the institutional church. Yet in the struggle to encounter the humanity that is mingled with spirituality, the seed is given sinew and strength. Often, just as the journey of the child in the womb is made possible by the care and love of those who travel with him, so the seed of faith in a new Christian is nurtured and strengthened by those who form the local community with whom the dangerous yet rewarding journey is to be taken.

The family goes to Bethlehem because they have no choice. The "powers that be" in every age always intrude on our humanity. Industry decides and a work force travels a thousand miles to find jobs. Governments legislate and laws are made. Computers revolve and our tax forms arrive. Always into the intimate Nazareths where we live, reaches the disturbing power of some distant Rome, demanding, directing, faceless.

Joseph is of Nazareth by all the practicalities of life, home, job, community involvement. But the computor says that by the legalities he is of Bethlehem. There is a providence that triumphs over the mundane decisions of bureaucracy, a destiny which has prepared this road to Bethlehem since the first moment of creation. What sometimes seems empty and pointless in the way that it directs our lives can offer new possibilities and reveal the design of God.

They come to an inn. There are lights, sounds, smells, loves, enmities, appetites, weariness, laughter, food and drink, sexuality, celebration, arguments, deals. On and on goes the whole spectrum of life. For this is the inn — the whole world, the global inn where we stay as guests and halt for a short while on our countless journeys through eternity.

The inn has no room for the child to be born. This is eternally and tragically true. For in the inn that is each one of us, there is constant holiday, constant crisis, constant distraction which crowds the rooms of our mind and heart and soul. Suddenly there is no room for anything except ourselves, our anxiety or passion or ambition. And at the gates of our consciousness, deep in our inmost being, God is offering us a new being to be born in the inn of our individual lives. But there is no room in the inn of our consciousness. It is too full of a thousand chattering guests. In his love God does not go away. Instead he goes, as we bid him, to a lower place, to the manger and the cave of our unconscious being, and there in the shadows he comes to birth.

The Searchers

Astrologers from the east arrived in Jerusalem, asking,
"Where is the child who is born to be king . . .
We observed the rising of his star."

Matthew 2:2

Every year, as surely as the season of the star comes around, the process of searching for an acceptable explanation begins. In planetariums there are special shows about the real astronomical facts behind the star of the Magi. The weekend supplements to newspapers produce annual articles in the same vein: the word used constantly is *real*. This suggests that the Bible story isn't really true but that there may be something real behind it, if only we can discover it with our modern scientific methods.

And yet the simple and profound image of the magi haunts us, simply because it communicates some beautiful and terrible truths. To be truly wise is to search for what is coming to birth in an age of death, to search for what is beginning anew in an age when much seems to be ending. To do this perturbs people. It perturbed Herod and indeed the whole of Jerusalem. Why? — because people easily become inured to death. They regard as normal many attitudes which are abnormal and spiritually malignant. It was normal in that long-ago world to see life as brutal and oppressive, to feel that history was static and imprisoned, just as it is normal to see our age as the prisoner of dark giants which stalk our consciousness and fill us with despair. In such a time it takes wise men and women to seek the child, the new life, the fresh possibility which God labours to bring to birth in the womb of the world.

There was Herod — there always is a "Herod" in human affairs. Herod is the entrenched position, the threatened structure, all that resents new possibilities and sets out to kill and stifle the process of birth. New birth in human affairs is disturbing because it is so unexpected. It upsets prearranged patterns. It refuses to conform. It is never born in our predictable Jerusalems or Caesareas where power and creativity are supposed to be in charge of production! Instead it sneaks into our world in the Bethlehems, in the backwaters, in human situations and in human minds where we presume that nothing can grow. The employee we always take for granted, the child we think of as slow, the marriage partner we find dull, the area of our own lives we see as stultifying — these are the Bethlehems which can blaze forth with unexpected glories.

But the travellers did not ask merely about the birth of a child. They asked about a child who would be king. Here lies the threat, and the promise, of what God brings to birth, whether it be in human affairs, human institutions, or human lives. When the new is born, and when it is of God, then it is king. It claims us, makes demands, forces change. He rules.

We always need our critical faculties when we search for the birth which God wishes for us and through us. The magi meet a ''Herod'' on the road to Bethlehem, a smiling, co-operative, fellow traveller on the search for the child. In our spiritual journeying there are such traps. There is the intense community which draws us until we realize that its very intensity will exhaust and destroy us. There is the fellowship which offers us certainty in return for total allegiance. There is the friend whose smiling euphoric piety masks a deep neurosis. Sometimes like those wise men of long ago we have to decide ''to return home another way.''

Above all, the wise men journeyed with their gifts. True wisdom sees life as a search for God, a search for the divine who waits to be born in each of us. And when we find him, and are found by him, we lay ourselves at the feet of God as a gift, because the offering of ourselves is the only real gift within our giving.

The Cost

Simeon blessed them and said to Mary his mother . . .
"You too shall be pierced to the heart."

Luke 2:34

Love is so costly. In the frantic and effervescent sixties there was a lapel button which was popular for a short while. It declared, "Love is damned hard work." It rang a note of truth and reality among the spasms and dreams of those years.

His mother communicates that to us — at least, through Luke's observant eye and ear. How quickly the girl becomes a woman, not so much prematurely old as prematurely wise. Perhaps that wisdom came from her perceptions about the cost of the joy and the life given to her. There is of course the cost that every woman knows — the slow inhabiting of one's body, the burden, sometimes the sickness, the approach of birth, the struggle, the gift of life, the mingled cries and tears and laughter. All that is the first cost. But also for her there is the coming of others into the stable and later into the house. There is the curiosity of locals, the strange visit of travellers with exotic gifts. Behind it all lurks a vague threat that the outside world is somehow involved with her child and is already inexplicably drawing him into its dangers and complexities and the moral labyrinth of its affairs. There too is cost, the cost and the threat which every parent feels.

Still recovering, her strength flowing back each day, she prepares to go where they must go, to the temple. They may be awed by the place, but they know what to do. Circumstances dictate a modest purchase for the sacrifice of thanksgiving for the boy's birth. Joseph buys the two birds, probably resenting the notoriously exorbitant price charged, and they present them, knowing that their gratitude and joy are beyond all price. Suddenly there is a feeling of other forces taking over again. The elderly Simeon reaches shakily but determinedly for the child. His fulsome words perhaps cause some embarrassment to the young couple as they anxiously watch the child in the old man's arms. Then comes the chill remark to his mother. "You too will be pierced to the heart." She knows a thrill of fear, made keener by her heightened feelings in this temple courtyard in this holiest of cities.

Every human being who has read this episode knows that all loving involves being "pierced to the heart" or else it is not loving. Parent and child, husband and wife, lover with lover, friend with friend — Simeon speaks to all of us until all time and loving end.

Time passes and joy is short lived. The vague threat of outside involvement, felt in the travellers with their gifts, suddenly becomes a terrible reality in Herod's crazy massacre. The journey that began at Nazareth with him in her womb now continues with him in her arms as the three of them desperately flee south-west to the desert and the comparative safety of Egypt.

They are eternal figures etched against a desert skyline in the evening. They are refugees, carrying a God who has accepted a refugee status. Century after century he will move across the world with refugees, fleeing from tyrants or war or famine. On every continent, in different ages and histories, his love will suffer with them, plead with them, often die with them. This is the eternal cost of that love which makes incarnation possible, the divine become human, the human become divine. There will of course be costs for Mary far beyond the end of this road to Egypt. She is the "Lady of Sorrows," the living embodiment of the costliness of all our loving.

The Encounter

When he was twelve...they made the pilgrimage as usual.
When the festive season was over... the boy Jesus
stayed behind in Jerusalem. His parents did not know.

Luke 2:42

He was twelve. Joseph was still alive and active. These were probably good years — enjoyable family life, satisfaction in seeing the boy help in the business, and the pleasure of watching him grow. Centuries later Christians were to have difficulty with the concept of his growing. The figure of the Lord Christ was to loom over and beyond the figure of the human being who breathed the country air of Galilee.

The joy and pain of growing are present not only for the person experiencing it, but also for those who have to look on from a distance. Typical of Luke's sensitivity to life is this brief glimpse which links the child of Bethlehem with the man of Nazareth. Here is the first of those inevitable moments remembered by all of us, when the growing and journeying of the emerging young person clashes with the anxiety and protectiveness of a parent. All of us have acted out this incident.

Significantly it happened on a journey, at a moment when his world was suddenly expanded by a visit to Jerusalem. And at the time Jerusalem was swollen and coloured with an element of cosmopolitanism created by the feast. It must have intoxicated that growing mind with endless possibilities, questions, and emotions. Until now he had known the rural world of Galilee, and was aware that, a few miles to the east, the great caravan highways swung around the lake and on to Damascus and beyond that to the infinitely remote orient. But never had he gone down that highway except in his imagination. He had lived in the familiar world of Nazareth, the sheltered home.

Even on this journey south the cocoon of the caravan gathered together and guarded the travellers through the lonely miles where the Pax Romana could not always prevent attack or robbery.

Now in this gleaming capital the wraps are taken off. The boy of Nazareth moves deeper into the labyrinth of city streets, mesmerized by the bustle and life. All the time he is drawn by something even he does not know. And at last he comes out on the great marble platform of Herod's temple. It is half a dozen modern city blocks long, terraced, battlemented, and higher than a Gothic cathedral of the Middle Ages. It gleams white in the Judean sun — for a Jewish boy the cradle of his civilization, the sacred centre of his inner universe.

There are voices, faces, questions, a welcome. He finds an instant rapport with the elders who detect something beyond definition in this wandering boy. And the hours go by as he discovers miles and endless miles of new country inside himself. Insights, ideas, horizons, all tumble and turn, calling him to a journey far beyond those few miles that he has already travelled. Suddenly, an interruption. Anxious, familiar faces appear, their voices sharpened by fear and exhaustion. And the boy, in turn, feels a flicker of resentment. The eternal cry of this encounter between youth and adult — Why don't they understand? Why can't they see that there is another parenthood than theirs, another voice that calls, another relationship that must be fulfilled and responded to.

Here is a quality we might pray to retain, a kind of spiritual youthfulness that is not immaturity. A spirituality which regards the city of God as perpetually exciting, perpetually waiting to be explored by each of us who are its pilgrims. A spirituality which continually seeks its inner temple and longs for deeper insights and deeper dialogue with our Father. A spirituality which nurtures and enriches, and enables us to return with new hope and energy to the Nazareths of our everyday existence, and to truly "advance in wisdom and in favour with God and man."

The Sounds of Silence

He went back with them to Nazareth . . .
As Jesus grew up he advanced in wisdom
and in favour with God and men.

Luke 2:51

Eighteen silent years for us as we try to follow him. And yet there are ways we can see him in those years from twelve to thirty, even without glimpses from any of the four evangelists. By inference we know many things. We know that he learned intimately the life of the hills and valleys of Galilee. All the vivid metaphors and captivating incidents by which he later describes "the kingdom," are flashes of those hidden years — the neighbour looking desperately for her lost coin, the shepherd leading the flock, the seed being sown in the field, the figs and olives gleaming in the hot sun.

We know that a deep intimacy with God somehow grew in him. Perhaps it began by an awareness of creation, that sweet pantheism that courses through our bodies and spirits as we move through adolescence to maturity, but it continued to a depth of intimacy which would allow him to speak of the God of creation in terms of childlike affection. He suggested years later that his followers call God *Abba*, not even the formal *Father* but more the equivalent of *Dad* or *Daddy*. It is intimacy and trust and love all mingled, the kind of relationship with God for which most of us long but only rarely capture.

We know that responsibilities increased for him. At some time he must have experienced the bereavement of Joseph's death and felt the trauma and sudden growing which that experience brings to everyone. We can go further and pay tribute to that quiet almost unknown man who lifted his child from the manger, taught him to walk, and guided his growing years. If the insights of modern psychology have any truth, Jesus' deep love of God as his Father, his concept of God as essentially loving, must have emerged to some degree from the relationship which existed between himself and Joseph in those Nazareth years. In Joseph God used an ordinary man to mirror the Fatherhood which lies at the heart of the created universe, and this fact takes us deep into our own lives. For there is a sense in which every act of parenting is potentially a mirror of Him of whom we are sons and daughters.

We know that there must have been questions about the future. What was ahead for a young man in that kind of world and time? Tides of resentment and rebellion swept across that little society, movements for social change began and disappeared, and all of them asked for involvement. Among these choices there was developing in him a sense of being called incessantly to do something and to be something, not only where he was but far beyond. He was haunted sometimes by the voice of Isaiah, which he would have learned as a boy in the synagogue. "The spirit of the Lord God is upon me because the Lord has anointed me; he has sent me to bring good news to the humble... to proclaim liberty to captives and release to those in prison; to proclaim a year of the Lord's favour" (Isaiah 61:1-2).

But what did it all mean? How did one take hold of it? How did one begin? No wonder the writer to the Hebrews was to say years after that "he had to be made like these brothers of his in every way... He is able to help those who are meeting their test now."

His first "being made like" us was in the growing and self-discovery of those years. In one sense we know nothing about them from any book. Yet there is a timeless book in which we can read and reach into the experience of our Lord — the book of our own growing! In the joy and pain of that personal story we discover the terrible humility of God who became one of us. And we come to realize that the process of our growing is in reality the process of our sanctification, if only we can see ourselves in him and he in us.

The River

*John the Baptist appeared in the wilderness proclaiming
a baptism... It happened at this time that Jesus came
from Nazareth in Galilee and was baptized.*

Mark 1:4

For a moment before he leaves Nazareth the veil is lifted. His
mother is now in our terms middle aged. In terms of his world
she is almost elderly. The calling and the haunting are about to
end, but this involves one more agonizing decision.

In the south, eighty or ninety miles away, a new voice is
attracting attention. It is harsh and strident yet commanding. It
speaks of a time for decision and commitment. In a distant sense
his own blood is calling, because John is his cousin. They call
him "the Baptizer," because he demands that simple but effective action as response to his message. In the brown swirling
river one falls back in trust on others. There is the momentary
panic of submersion, the flash of death, and then the drawing of
breath again in the bright sunlight, a sense of newness, of rising,
of birth!

Do you leave Nazareth for that? Do you listen to those who
say that it is just another movement that risks temple condemnation or Roman spears? Do you feel responsibility to those who
depend on your work financially? Is this the call you've been
expecting, or is it a delusion to be avoided? The decision to go,
the going itself, were both costly. And so he came to the place, a
stranger, as all Galileans were in this blazing hot valley leading
to the Dead Sea. Their eyes met and the longing for certainty in
Jesus' eyes is mirrored by an ambivalence in John's. But for both
of them it is beyond going back. They move into the water.

Luke gropes for words as we will always have to. Presumably
Jesus related the experience more than once. When he comes up
from that transitory burial under the water, it seems as if his
world ignites and shines with validation and certainty. He is
right! The journey has brought him home! Wave upon wave of
peace and wholeness descend on him, calming, resolving, dove-
like. Thundering in his consciousness are the intimations of the
truth about himself and his vocation. He feels the affirmation

and the terror of being in the presence of him by whom he is called my Son, my Beloved.

We all know the agony of leaving our Nazareths. We know the ambivalence of all decisions, all encounters with change. We know those moments when conversations and advice must end and when we must decide for ourselves. We have all walked the hilly miles to the place of decision and commitment, and have experienced moments when our heavens opened and the dove descended and there sounded the inner voice of validation and acceptance.

And perhaps, most important, we will have that experience again, because the saying of our Yes, the ending of the search, the alighting of the dove, is something that must be experienced again and again if life is to retain energy, openness, horizons. In our spirituality, in our work, in our relationships, we are always approaching boundaries of partial growth and achievement. But we have a choice. We can stop at the boundary, put down our roots and opt for Nazareth. Or we can decide to go further, further into a particular relationship, further in our self-giving and self-revealing. We may choose to go elsewhere, in some other direction in our work, or deeper in our spirituality. In doing so we choose to leave our Nazareths.

And here is a mystery. The love of God sometimes allows us to choose and at other times seems to allow us no choice, but drags us kicking and screaming to the river of our self-discovery and our peace.

The Wilderness

Full of the Holy Spirit... (Jesus) was led...
up and down the wilderness and tempted by the devil.

Luke 4:1

Beyond the river of decision lies the wilderness of implementation. It did for Jesus, and it does for all of us. For him, getting to the place of baptism is a struggle. Choosing to come south from Nazareth, choosing to make a commitment to John's message rather than to other things that called for a like commitment — all this is a struggle. And having made the choice, he experiences deep peace and validation. There is, as Luke tells us, the Dove descending and the Voice declaring his identity.

When Jesus began his work he was about thirty years old. But we can only begin our work, whoever we are and whatever the work is, when we know who we are. As soon as we make that beginning, we face choices about implementing our own decision, and choices often mean wilderness. But the wilderness is solitary, and the choices have often to be made alone.

The other significant element in Jesus' experience is that he goes into the wilderness full of the Holy Spirit. Many find this difficult to admit, as if it is letting God down. But the experience of the Holy Spirit, however affirming and strengthening it may be, does not spare us from turmoil, choice, anxiety — wilderness. Our being given grace, perhaps in some experience of God's reality and presence, may be a resource for dealing with the wilderness, for surviving in it, but not necessarily a means of avoiding it.

Knowing that the wilderness cannot be avoided, Jesus moves into it. There is no Olympian calm about him. Luke says that he moved "up and down." There is a hint of the restless, a pacing tension which we all know. Which way lies an answer? Which direction should be followed? Which voice should be listened to?

In the wilderness is the demon who, appearing in many shapes, speaking with different voices, offers endless options. The first tactic of our demon is often to fascinate us by the choices themselves. One can spend endless time in the game of deciding the next step, and thus avoid the step itself! Self-analysis is a vast industry. Our motivations, our own development, our identity problems can fascinate us for as long as we allow them. Jesus then, in this process of temptation, of choosing one among many options, is acting out our own humanity. Shall it be stones turned into bread? Will that effect the creation of a new movement towards what — revolution? Shall it be a display of superman qualities from the temple height? Shall it be a total acceptance of the political process, the strategic alliance, the accumulation of power and influence, the "kingdom of the world" as Luke puts it? What is significant is the common thread. The demon says, "Effect your plans by means of power. Show your strengths. Develop an image of power whether or not it be a reality of power, and the image will become self fulfilling."

But Jesus refuses the way which depends on a display of power. He returns from the wilderness because the choice has been made. He turns toward the home country of Galilee, and he seeks out all the familiar that is there — the intimate, the vulnerable, the limited, the human. And finding them he says, "Follow me." He rejects the way of power and chooses the way of relationship; he rejects the mob waiting to be led and chooses instead the community waiting to be shared. And so beside the lake the decision taken in the wilderness is implemented. Two friends are called from their nets, and they in turn call others. Unlike the kingdoms of earth which are stormed by arms, this kingdom is discovered in eyes meeting, hands touching, hearts experiencing.

So it is always. We enter our wilderness and discover the demons of insecurity, time pressures, hyper-tension, self-doubt. Their name is Legion. And yet other demons make us feel that the only way out is by our own powers, our self-centered objectives, our ability to overcome and crush others. The latter is sometimes presented to us in the temptation of leading them. If we are wise, we recall the One who walked this echoing shrieking wilderness before us. The remembrance of him may make it possible for us to see that whoever God wishes us to become we can achieve most richly *with* others rather than *over* them, with love rather than with power, in community rather than in solitary prominence. When we hear and listen to these voices in the wilderness, when we decide to follow them, we know that in the wilderness, among the demons, dwell also our angels.

Andrew and Simon

Two disciples... followed Jesus... He asked,
"What are you looking for?" They said, "Rabbi,
where are you staying?" "Come and see," he replied.

John 1:37

He built the community so simply. At least it seems simple in the terse, economic narrative of Matthew. There on the beach at the north end of the lake near Capernaum, they were mending their nets. It was probably evening. And out of the evening sun, pouring across the hills and the lake, he drew near. He said to them, "Come with me," and they followed.

John recalls it all differently. For him the memory of that first meeting is centered at Bethany (not the village near Jerusalem which meant so much to Jesus later on, but beyond or east of the Jordan). Two men were already involved in a search for some focus in their lives. They had linked up with John the Baptist, preaching in the area. And suddenly Jesus passed by. It may well have taken place in that interim between his experience of wrestling in the desert and his decision to head north for Galilee again. The two men were intrigued by John's hint that there was something tremendously significant about this man passing by. They began to walk after the disappearing figure. They began to catch up with him. Suddenly Jesus turned and asked a simple but timeless and thought-provoking question. He said, "What are you looking for?"

How do you answer that? He asks it again and again of us, and we react as they did. We have no real answer. We stumble and say inane things. We try to change the conversation. They said to him, "Where are you staying?" It wasn't a reply but the postponement of a reply, an admission that there can be no reply. And yet they didn't seem like fools. God's questions to us may sometimes show our human foolishness, but they are not designed to make us feel foolish. Instead they suddenly show us things about ourselves which we badly need to deal with. We want to know where the asker of the question is staying, because we want to remain in his presence if only to discover hidden areas of ourselves. We always want to stay longer with someone whose insight is willing to probe us and show us ourselves.

The invitation is the easiest imaginable. Jesus says to them, "Come and see." In its quality of ease and gentleness and lack of coercion, it echoes that other sentence he would use later by the lake further north, "Follow me." In its capacity to allow the invited person total freedom to choose, it is opposite to all the ways suggested by the demon in the desert. Those were to bribe, to impress, to dominate. This is the way of freedom, of respect for others.

We know one of the two men involved in that tentative and gentle conversation. He was Andrew. He went and told his brother Peter, and Peter came and met this fellow Galilean who possessed a peculiar serenity and authority and insight. Before he left next day for Galilee they had him meet another friend named Philip, and he in turn involved Nathanael. The latter responded grumpily, but came and felt that same tantilizing attraction. And then they said goodbye, and he headed north. No promises were given and none were asked. No arrangement was made to meet. They were free, free to choose, free to follow.

Eventually they too went north again, homeward to the lake and their fishing. They couldn't live on the wind then, and we still can't. But this isn't the point. Sometimes beyond the day to day events and responsibilities, there are things which won't stop haunting us, demanding to be dealt with. They went back to fishing, and he possibly returned west across the rolling hills to Nazareth, to check the family shop. Weeks went by, maybe months. We do not know whether they met and talked during that time, but one thing we do know. There came an evening when the nets were spread and talk went on and the water slapped against the quay wall, and he came to them. Perhaps there were some passing who noticed the five men talking, (six if James and John's father Zebedee happened to be there). A little later the sun was lower across the lake, and only the old man was left passing the nets through his gnarled hands. The others had gone with the carpenter from Nazareth. They did not yet know it, but they were the first of the community which he had come to create.

If we choose, we can walk with them in that same community which, like him, is "the same yesterday, today, and forever."

Call and Response

The next day Jesus decided to leave for Galilee.

John 1:43

He gathered twelve of them, not all at the same time. First there were four, and later they followed one by one. We don't know the precise circumstances. For instance, we can never be bystanders at that ironic and tragic moment when Judas said, "Yes," probably with the best intentions and the most genuine commitment. It may just be too simple to presume that a Yes came out of one meeting with a stranger. Life isn't really like that for most of us. We have some hints that it may not have been like that for them. Matthew tells us years afterwards that Jesus met Andrew and Simon by the lake at Capernaum (Matthew 4:18). On the other hand John seems to say that Andrew met Jesus when they were both down south at the Jordan listening to the fiery preaching of John the Baptist (John 1:40). Andrew then brought Simon.

It is not at all contradictory. How totally natural it would have been for their Yes to have formed in the following days and weeks, chatting with him in the Jordan area while he gathered his strength and his thoughts after that time in the wilderness across the river, or travelling north with him, and others, who had come down from the lake country. As a matter of fact we know definitely that there were others down for a visit. John tells of Philip and Nathanael being there too. Perhaps they decided gradually as they headed home. Perhaps they weren't even aware what they would do, until the day he met them again in their familiar surroundings and asked them to follow him.

There was wisdom in not asking them for a Yes away from home. When we are in unfamiliar surroundings, we sometimes do unreal things and make unreal commitments. We feel ourselves to be different people. We decide and act differently, and sometimes everything looks quite different when we return home. But if the decision can be made again at home and confirmed there, then it is real. So they chatted down south, but it was back home that he uttered those two momentous words, "Follow me."

Follow to where? Up and down the country? Not a very precise program. To Jerusalem? Not a pleasant prospect for northern fishermen. To death? God forbid. To resurrection? What does that mean? You just respond to him. Why? You don't know. Something draws you beyond yourself, away from the boat, away from the job, away from the town. Afterwards you realize that maybe you should have asked a few questions, or asked for some guarantees. But for some reason you didn't. In the months that followed there were moments of second thoughts when you did ask for an explanation. Those were the times when you felt you were following in the dark and God knows where it was all going to end.

Today we love to make what sociological jargon calls "contracts." If I do X what will you do? If I give you this will you give me that? The encounter on the lake long ago would seem to come very short of our modern calculated contracts. And yet the deepest commitments we make are usually like that long ago Yes of those men. You say it because you have to. It's drawn out of you. To use other language, it transcends you. You realize that there is a Thou calling to your I. It may be in matters of friendship, sexuality, commitment to marry. It may be between you and the Christ who encounters you today as surely as a friend named Jesus encountered those men then.

Months after that meeting by the lake he would remind them of their Yes. He would point out something they may never have realized and may well have been very surprised at, as we are surprised when he says it to us. He said, "You did not choose me: I chose you."

Ordinary Men

Scripture says, "I will destroy the wisdom of the wise"...
God has made the wisdom of this world look foolish.

I Cor. 1:19

C.S. Lewis has an unforgettable passage in *The Screwtape Letters*. Two devils are discussing how to wreck the new Christian faith of a young person. The old devil exhorts the other to get the man to church; then all the ordinary people he sees will be so different from the romantic and idealistic images of Christians which he has in his mind that his faith will be shattered. And off he will go to look for the beautiful and the perfect and the noble elsewhere.

That's what strikes you about the people Jesus chose. At first glance they are devastatingly ordinary. All of them, with the possible exception of Judas, came from the familiar rural world of Galilee. All of them were perfectly aware of the huge and complex world around them, but there is no evidence that any of them had experienced it. In that sense they were ordinary men. There is no record that a single one of them was in any way particularly noted for his religious piety, for his intellectual standing, or for anything at all. Today their figures grace the stained glass windows of countless cathedrals and churches. Their names loom large in the world's religious memory. Yet a look at the human being behind what has become a symbol is very salutary. The list of their names actually can bring to mind a certain number of characteristics and incidents which are far from inspiring.

Peter seems to spend a great deal of his time groping emotionally and clumsily for some understanding of what Jesus is about, so much so that his misdirected concern draws a sharp and exasperated rebuke from Jesus. James and John betrayed a total lack of understanding about their master in their selfish request for a high position in whatever good things were coming. Jesus returns from the mountain of the transfiguration to find a screaming child surrounded by his disciples, concerned, frustrated, totally ineffective. On the way to Jerusalem when a blind beggar cries for attention, the disciples only tell him to "shut up."

In the garden of Gethsemane, in the ensuing trial, even at Calvary itself, the disciples with two known exceptions, Peter and John, are at least very distant and possibly totally absent. In the presence of the risen Lord, just before that mysterious moment of withdrawal which we call the Ascension, they ask him a question which reveals their inability, even at this point, to grasp what those months with him have been about.

All of this should jolt us into the joyful realization that if we sometimes writhe under the feeling that our own discipleship is very uninspired and ordinary, we are in very good company! The contribution made by those closest to Jesus ranged from total misunderstanding, naked selfishness, to deepest betrayal. This ordinariness is an ironic thread running through the New Testament. It is one of the jokes which God plays on our human expectations, one of the ways in which he shows us that his thoughts are not our thoughts and his ways are not our ways.

We see this best if we look a little longer at Peter. Many years after the crucifixion and resurrection, when the early Christian communities were scattered across the Roman Empire, Peter had become indeed a rock, as Jesus had said he would, to whom many of those communities looked for strength. Yet a reading of Peter's letter to those other Christians reveals a simplicity, a kind of down-to-earth quality which is the legacy of that long ago lakeside community.

One paragraph in that letter shows this quality particularly. Peter is writing to many people who are desperately trying to construct a workable style of life in a growingly complex, threatening, and depressing world. But look at what Peter suggests — "lead an ordered and sober life given to prayer ... keep your love for one another at full strength ... be hospitable ... Whatever gift each of you may have received, use it in service to one another... In all things so act that the glory may be God's through Jesus Christ" (I Peter 4:7).

There it is, perfectly straightforward and understandable, in one sense, quite ordinary. Yet in that long ago darkening period of history, and in this equally darkening period of history which is our time, that deceptively ordinary pattern for living can transform life from emptiness to meaning, from despair to joy.

The Wedding

There was a wedding in Cana in Galilee.
Jesus and his disciples were guests.

John 2:1

We knocked at the door of the small Franciscan church in Cana.
The tiny courtyard was empty. It was late afternoon. At the
window there was a movement; a hand waved. A few moments
later a small and smiling brown-robed welcomer let us in. After
we had chatted about many things, his eyes twinkled and he
said, "Now, would you like a glass of water which has been
changed into wine?" and, together, we drank. Behind the jest he
was pointing out a truth. Year by year God is always turning
water into wine. From a thousand seas and lakes and rivers,
from ten thousand vineyards, the blood-red beauty flows and
splashes and sparkles.

Cana is only a few miles across the hills from Nazareth. The
family might well have been relatives. In the simple statement
of John that "the mother of Jesus was there," we have an
ominous hint that Joseph by this time was dead. It is significant
that "Jesus and his disciples were guests;" they were already
seen as a group, a teacher with his disciples.

This is the first moment in which we see him with his mother
at the time of his maturity. The girl Mary and the child are gone.
Images of madonnas no longer suffice. This is the far more subtle
business of adult relationships across the generations. A woman
and her adult son are really four people. To her there is a child
and a man. To him there is a mother and a middle-aged woman.
Every conversation is held on all those levels. There is always
the need for sensitivity, always the possibility of hurt.

The social crisis is dealt with. Glasses are filled and raised.
There is laughter and congratulation. And the story will be told
again and again; it will echo and re-echo among those who seek
him as Lord long after his suffering, death, and resurrection.
The story is taken and used to teach a truth. It is placed in the
gospel. It is deepened and enriched by the context of faith.

In this story of a wedding long ago, on an altar, still and deep
in its chalice, wine is a thing of many meanings. Withdraw from
the village of Cana, leave that long ago century, tell the story out

of its culture and time... The wedding is life itself, its celebration, its companionship, its rhythms, purposes, and decisions. In that living there are times when the laughter dies, when the wine of joy and celebration, energy and hope runs out. And in its place is a kind of water which seems grey and bland. Existence at such times becomes drab, shadowy, depressing. Yet the Christ of faith takes us to the shadowed waters which seem so insufficient to nourish our lost hope and joy. He helps us face their plainness and ordinariness and lack of inspiration, makes us look into their depths, and in so doing shows us how to use these seeming ordinary and everyday elements of our experience to change our lives.

In Christ many have found it possible to change the waters of emptiness into the wine of joy and hope and meaning. And very often as we taste this newly discovered wine, we discover it to be more than the wine of our previous experience. The more our life proceeds, the more frequently we experience the water of life being turned to new wine. The more this happens the more we realize something about that wine which he gives us for our strengthening. We realize that it is no longer the sparkling and bubbly light wine of our earlier experience but is now mingled with the blood, sweat, and tears of our own growing and of his self-giving to us. It is rich and powerful wine, and to touch it to our lips is to taste moments of depth and grace and power. We know we are tasting the wine of him who keeps the good wine to the last.

Levi

Jesus saw a man named Matthew at his seat
in the custom house, and said to him, "Follow me;"
and Matthew rose and followed him.

Matthew 9:9

He had very cleverly placed his office where he could see everything. You could never slip into the jetty and get rid of some or
all of a good catch without being seen. The jetties and quaysides
of Capurnaum were a hive of activity. Soldiers from the army on
their daily beat through the town, servants from nearby farms
buying fresh fish for a banquet, fishermen trying to get a good
price for the night's catch and sometimes showing the impa-
tience of weariness as they longed to get home to sleep. Watching
it all from his office window was Levi.

Being a tax collector gives you choices. You can throw caution
and friendship to the wind and squeeze plenty out of people. Or
you can be reasonable, give the authorities what they demand,
and live decently off the rest. This much people understand and
perhaps grudgingly accept. But someone else is watching the
proceedings on the quayside. A certain man from Nazareth is
abroad, and small groups are meeting in a couple of the local
houses. It is possible that he and Levi have spoken a number of
times — nothing lengthy or intimate, perhaps odd moments of
sizing each other up during casual conversation. One day a figure
passes the small window overlooking the quayside. A moment
later it blocks the light from the door and sends deep shadows
over Levi's neatly written column of weights and amounts.

Whether Levi actually walked out of his office there and then
matters not. But it may well be that he often looked back to that
moment as the time when something ended and something
began. Life is often like that; its dividing lines appear clear and
neat only in retrospect. But that was the moment when Levi
said, "Yes," probably like the rest of them, not knowing quite
what he was saying Yes to, but knowing only a person who called
and who had to be followed. It changed him deeply and forever.
He expressed that change in his name. Because he always felt
that the encounter was worth more than all the calculations and

contracts in his ledgers, he saw it as a gift beyond price. So he became Matthew, which means "God's Gift."

To the extent that we possess intimations and yearnings for God, we are all Matthew. Yearning for God is his gift to us. There are rare souls, not necessarily brilliant or academic or saintly in the accepted sense, who possess certainties, who walk with God for much of their life. But most of us discover God only in moments of presence and flashes of insight. Yet these moments and flashes mean that we have been encountered by One who is offering us the gift of himself. It means that, as for Levi on the quayside of Capernaum, there is one who approaches and speaks and withdraws again, waiting for our response.

From our side response is the beginning of our gift giving. Levi becomes Matthew not only because he realizes that Jesus has come as a gift to him, but because he in turn has offered himself as a gift to Jesus. One of the unbelievable facts in the relationship between Christ and men and women is that the process of our giving ourselves is done in total freedom. We can withhold ourselves. Levi did not lay down his pen and book in a hypnotic trance. His allegiance was not forced. He did not become less Levi by becoming Matthew. Rather for the first time he recognized with blinding clarity the Levi part of him and accepted it as good material from which something else could be created.

The call of Levi, the change to Matthew, made eyes widen and tongues wag in that long ago community. Whenever a Levi becomes a Matthew it always astonishes us. At a party in Levi's house Jesus was questioned on this seeming strangeness of his choice. His answer, which we are continually forgetting, was "I did not come to invite virtuous people, but sinners."

Meeting Places

Here I stand knocking at the door; if anyone hears my voice and opens the door, I will come in.

Revelation 3:20

If you leaf through a bundle of New Yorker magazines you notice how frequently the cartoons are set in business offices. Usually they show up some very personal foible in the otherwise dignified or powerful businessman. Why is this particularly amusing? Perhaps it is because personal foibles are what we try to keep hidden in the private area of our lives. At work we are often in public. We wear special clothes, and we think and behave differently than we do at home.

It is very difficult to place words like *business* and *job* beside *religion* and *faith*. Very often we work down-town, and the church is in the suburbs. Religion concerns home and family and the private area. Business concerns the office or the shop and our public existence. All of this is questioned by a careful reading of the Bible. If we observe not only the life of our Lord Jesus but many other stories in the Old Testament, we find the richest episodes are those that tell how people have been encountered by God and caught by him. The fascinating thing is that almost all such incidents occur during the pursuit of ongoing responsibilities, in other words *at work!*

Moses is carrying out the tasks of a shepherd in the harshest of settings, and there he is intrigued by a bush that burns. Something he has been trying for a long time to push away comes forward with an ultimate demand. His whole life changes.

Nehemiah is an exile in Babylon working on the king's personal staff. Among the ceaseless demands of high responsibility, comes the demand of God, and in the midst of his most public existence, Nehemiah responds.

Peter and Andrew are thigh deep in the slime and chill of a fishing boat when a figure approaching along the lakeshore issues an invitation to follow him. Whether or not the boat was suddenly bereft of owners (because there is ample evidence that they frequently needed it again), their lives were immediately changed.

Levi is assiduously scribbling tax entries in his ledger when he looks up into what may well have been a familiar face and finds himself responding to a course of action beyond his wildest imagination.

Paul is totally committed to the preservation of public security and morality. He is an apt symbol of contemporary man because he is not even in his office but travelling! His world and experience would today include an expensive brief-case, a travelling alarm clock, and a big, impressive file. Suddenly another reality slices through the professional armour, and Paul is on his knees listening to directions which would seem highly unsatisfactory and imprecise to his former professional instincts. "Get up," he is told, "Go into the city, and you will be told what you have to do."

The Bible is full of such incidents which tell repeatedly how human beings experience the presence of God at their places of public involvement. This does not for a moment deny that the Bible is just as open to the possibility of God speaking within the private place, the quiet moment, the contemplative experience, the sacred building. But the danger in our Western world is to draw our well beloved lines of demarcation on the movements of God, defining where he has the right to appear, to confront, or to invite. As we furnish our offices with desks and our kitchens with counters, God knows that a desk and a counter are both potential altars.

The Storm

*He was in the stern asleep on a cushion; they roused him
and said, "Master, we are sinking! Do you not care!"*

Mark 4:38

For most seasons of the year the lake is still, reflecting on one
side the quayside and buildings of towns like Tiberias and on the
other the steep hillsides of the Golan. At the north end is all that
is left of Capernaum. Here on a wooded shore the water laps
quietly. But this can change. The cats paws of the first flurry,
the swift lifting of the water to choppiness, then the white caps
slapping and leaping against the small wharfside. In the driving
rain the distant heights of the Golan disappear. You are alone in
the storm.

He liked going over to the other side, to the eastern shore that
even today is for the most part sparsely populated. For it meant
escape, a break from the incessant drain of people, a time to be
alone, and most of all, a time to be with his Father in prayer. As
they sailed along he went to sleep. Probably he was bone weary.
That should fill us with awe because of its indications of his utter
humanity. Our sleep is a telling of our own humanity. We
acknowledge dependence, vulnerability, finitude. Our muscles,
symbols of our pitiful illusion of strength and control, relax and
sag. Our faces no longer project the image we wish. Sleep reveals
us completely.

So God in human flesh sleeps. His limbs curl up in the limited
space of the fishing boat, his head droops, his jaw sags. He may
even have snored! He is so weary that he doesn't wake as the
motion of the boat changes, as men begin to mutter their concern, clamber about to change a sail, or shout orders as the
squall fills the sail with a crack and the rain slashes down.
Through all this he doesn't wake.

There are times when God seems to be asleep. As long as the
afternoon of our adult life is still and the surface of events over
which we move is smooth, we are seemingly sufficient to cope.
Our muscles can row, our eyes can guide, our heads can plan.
But when the thunderclap of disaster sounds, the thick fog of
depression or indecision rolls in, the cold lash of pain drenches
and numbs the senses, then we have the feeling that God sleeps.

Out on the lake a shout goes up. They are sinking — the timeless cry of humanity. It wells up from human lives, from human relationships, from human institutions, from human civilizations — especially when it seems that everything has been tried and nothing has worked. Some feel only contempt for that cry sounded, they say, against an empty universe. Others realize that the cry can signal a moment of change, of turning, of recovery, of new creation. The cry for help, the acknowledgement of need, the realization of one's inability to handle things — this heralds the beginning of the new. But there is an even deeper and more subtle truth demonstrated in this moment of desperation on the lake. It is easily missed, as many deep human feelings are, when we read or listen. They said to him, ''Do you not care?''

In hospital rooms, beside graves, when disaster strikes, pain gathers, or hope dies — in all these moments we have cried out, ''Do you not care?'' There are such moments of screaming anger at God, and often we feel guilty when we have vented our emotions. Yet resentment against God is a most legitimate part of our humanity. It is all through the Bible story: Moses roaring his exasperation, Elijah yelling his self-pity and sense of betrayal, Jeremiah crying out in an agony of resentment about his vocation — and the common theme is, ''Do you not care?'' In the venting of our anger there is a cleansing, a stilling and a peace, and we come after the storm to a place where prayers can be said and the presence of Another is found.

Peter

*(Andrew) brought Simon to Jesus, who looked at him
and said, "You are Simon, son of John.
You shall be called Cephas" (that is, Peter, the Rock).*

John 1:42

It is easy to forget that the Bible is rich not only in triumphant
moments and incidents in human life but also in moments of
utter and abject failure. It is also probably true that these latter
moments have proved the richest source of our inspiration. In
the average life there are very few occasions when we identify
with triumph, and frequently there are occasions when we
know, if not failure, at least the fear of it.

The man who more than any other gospel character personifies
our humanity is Simon Peter. The genius of the Western church
in placing him at the heart of its history rests in his real humanity. And the richness issuing from that humanity can be expressed
only in paradox — strength from weakness, insight from blind-
ness, nobility from betrayal, courage from cowardice. When we
can free ourselves from looking at Simon Peter as a great historic
figure, as a saint enshrined in stained glass or a character in
sacred scripture, and instead begin to look at him as the fisher-
man of Capernaum, the friend of Jesus, and the leader of the
Christian community, then we can see a man who was an extra-
ordinary mixture of failure and success.

Within minutes at Caesarea Philippi he earns Jesus' fervent
gratitude and then his stern rebuke. In a lakeside episode he
reacts with total spontaneity to the approach of Jesus across the
water, and leaps overboard only to find that he has to be rescued.
In later life Peter reveals all the ambivalence felt in the early
Christian community about the traditional Jewish dietary laws.
On one side he is drawn towards a liberal stance by his vision in
Joppa, and on the other he is fiercely taken to task by Paul for
refusing to eat with those outside the tradition of Israel. Even
this list does not exhaust the occasions on which this most
human of men revealed the strange mixture that he was. Yet we
look with growing respect as time goes by, and we watch Jesus'
confidence in Peter begin to be rewarded.

The pivotal moment in this process is recounted by Luke, who lifts the curtain and allows us to be among the group in the Upper Room. On that never-to-be-forgotten night Jesus turned to Peter and said something which must have chilled him. "Simon, take heed," said Jesus, "Satan has been given leave to sift all of you like wheat... (but) when you have come to yourself, you must lend strength to your brothers" (Luke 22:31).

As we know only too well, each one of them around that table was going to be sifted like wheat, their resilience tested to the uttermost, and most of them were going to break under pressure. They would leave Jesus alone in the hands of his captors. They would crouch behind locked doors in total disarray. In some ways Peter was to buckle under that terrible sifting. During the dark hours when he was making his way from the hillside, tracing the way Jesus had been taken until he came to the lights of the high priest's house in the southern end of the city, what gave Peter the courage to stay nearby may have been the memory of Jesus' words a few hours before the supper. "Simon, for you I have prayed that your faith may not fail."

When it was all over, or we might choose to say when it was all about to begin, when the unbelievable joy of the risen Presence had been tasted, we see the rock-like nature of Peter begin to emerge. Later in the New Testament we see him as the respected leader of the scattered Christian communities. Peter may often have recalled Jesus' words. He may have realized what many have realized since, that the capacity to be strong most often comes from those who have known what it is to be weak, to feel drained and sifted through the cold fingers of suffering and fear and failure. Peter may often have realized with amazement and gratitude that to Jesus it was almost irrelevant that he should fail.

Failure is almost taken for granted in our human make-up. The magnificent assurance is that the capacity for strengthening others can often emerge from our own experience of weakness and failure. As the lordship of the risen Christ emerges from the cross, so the human capacity to be healers ourselves emerges from the wounds we already bear.

47

The Mountain Top

Peter said to him, "Master, how good it is
that we are here! Shall we make three shelters!"...
but he spoke without knowing what he was saying.

Luke 9:33

In every community, however healthy and loving its relationships, there are degrees of intimacy. Nobody can like or feel
close to everyone else with total impartiality. In the small
community of disciples to which Christians look back, it was
no different. If we accept the full humanity of Jesus, then we
accept the fact that he too felt degrees of closeness in his relationships.

There are a number of occasions when three disciples seem to
have formed a kind of inner circle. These were Peter, James, and
John. At a certain stage in the community's life, when they may
have been together for about eighteen months, Jesus moved
toward an incident in his life which has become for Christians
one of the most beautiful and mysterious points of focus. We do
not know exactly where these few days were spent. These four
companions may have headed north-east to the slopes of Mount
Hermon, topped with its year-round snowy peak. Or perhaps
they took the short, steep climb up nearby Mount Tabor, which
rises a few miles from Nazareth and dominates the whole of
Galilee. But in whatever direction they went, Jesus took the
particular three who meant so much to him.

We can't really follow them up those slopes. We have been
told what happened in the words of tradition passed on by the
early Christian communities. But even by that time the story
had acquired symbolic meaning, as do past incidents in our own
lives. And what of us who presume in our fragile and groping
way to be his disciples? What moments of transfiguration can
we claim or expect or pray for? In what direction lie our spiritual
horizons, and how are they to be reached? In what direction is
our Mount Hermon or our Mount Tabor? Do we not have to consider also that not all disciples are taken up the mountains of
transfiguration?

To this last there is no answer. I suspect that most of us glimpse
the spiritual heights not because we have climbed them, but

because in the beauty and sanctity of another's life we have glimpsed a peak high beyond the lower slopes where we do most of our own journeying. Andrew was Peter's brother, yet he never himself saw that blinding light, never trembled before the thunder, never looked into familiar eyes and saw a terrible, unfamiliar majesty shining out of them. Most of us are Andrew rather than Peter. Yet Andrew remained faithful, remained part of the community, and went on to be one of the giants around which the faith evolved and spread and deepened. Why? Because of what he sensed radiating from his brother, who after that experience was the same and yet was different. His brother was, in some hard to define way, changed — a kind of lesser transfiguration.

We discover our mountains of transfiguration in much the same way. Sometimes we find them, if they are granted to us, in a blinding moment of conversion, in a moment of realizing the presence and reality of God, in a moment of realizing the truth and call of Christ, in a moment of sacramental meeting, when the bread in our hands and the wine on our lips suddenly acquires a flavor and a vintage which takes us out of time and out of our human limitations and intoxicates us with God. All these moments are known and described many times in Christian history and spirituality.

Yet they are moments given to those who are invited or who stumble on the way to the mountain. But what is the way? Where is the gate in the wall of everyday experience which opens onto the mountains of God? It's significant that in all the great stories of the world where heroes and heroines search for the path to the secret places of God the entrance is disguised. It will be a certain cave hidden by a rock. In C.S. Lewis' *Chronicles of Narnia* it will be the door of an old wardrobe in an attic room.

The path leading to the mountain of our transfiguration begins in the unsuspected and the ordinary — the relationship which we feel has become humdrum, the task which we resent, the individual who suddenly displays an unexpected greatness and courage and faith which blinds us and fills us with awe and makes us realize that we both stand in a greater presence. These are the secret and unexpected openings that lead to the path by which we eventually stand on the mountain of life's transfiguration.

Zacchaeus

There was a man there named Zacchaeus;
he was superintendent of taxes and very rich...
but, being a little man, he could not see (Jesus)
for the crowd...

Luke 19:2

The Roman tax system was simple, cynical, and effective. Its method was to gouge as much as possible from as many people as possible. Its objective was to keep the lumbering machinery of empire, particularly the army, functioning. The diabolically clever refinement of the system was that whenever possible subjects were taxed by one of their own people. To achieve this the office of tax collector was put out on what we would today call a tender. It went to the highest bidder who then, knowing exactly how much he had paid out for the doubtful privilege, proceeded to collect more than that in taxes from his fellows. It was not an unpleasant occupation so long as you did not mind being the social outcast of your community and sometimes walking in fear of your life.

Zacchaeus who lived in Jericho, was a tax collector — affluent, lonely, held in general contempt. He was not of course without allies; the Romans protected their agents. All of which would further alienate his fellow countrymen by adding fear to their contempt. Zacchaeus typifies that figure who turns up again and again in scripture — the outsider, the person who for one reason or another looks in from the edge but must always stay there. It is on the edge that we meet him, shut out by others, desperately anxious to be part of the proceedings, and failing.

With typical sensitivity Luke mentions that Zacchaeus was a little man. There is a kind of littleness which is far more devastating and corroding than the merely physical. This diminishment emerges from one's self image, and in turn is reflected in the attitudes of others toward us. We are all at our most vulnerable here. Subject to others' like and dislike, approval or disapproval, we suffer a thousand diminishments and enjoy a thousand growings. Lewis Carrol, in that most adult of so-called children's books *Alice in Wonderland*, depicts Alice at a certain stage in her adventures growing and growing until her head hits the ceiling, whereupon she shrinks and shrinks almost to the vanishing point.

Zacchaeus would have known that feeling. And Luke expresses it perfectly by putting side by side two deceptively ordinary statements. Zacchaeus, Luke says, was "very rich" yet he was "a little man."

Zacchaeus feels impelled to catch a glimpse of the stranger in Jericho. Jesus is all that he is not. Jesus is admired, sought out, and above all, accepted. How often in our loneliness or alienation, in our real or imagined non-acceptance, we long to identify with someone else's obvious acceptance. We look from a distance, like Zacchaeus in his tree, imprisoned in our loneliness, envy, and self pity. Suddenly the utterly unexpected happens. An invitation is given. More, a favour is asked, the most intimate favour of hospitality. When it is requested of Zacchaeus, who has grown so accustomed to being shunned, he is beside himself with excitement. In the ensuing encounter all the masks are taken off, all the walls he had so carefully built around himself are broken down.

Significantly the result is not shame but joy. Zacchaeus is stripped naked by the encounter, but he is dancing not cowering. He is dancing because he is somehow for the first time free. Part of his joy and freedom is in the realization that finally someone fully aware of who and what he is has accepted him without conditions.

Confession, even as a word, has a terror about it. It smacks of courts and judges. It has a medieval sternness, a religious chill. Yet tasted in actuality and carried out in circumstances where we know that we are completely accepted, affirmed, and loved — all of which is true of God's stance toward us — the elements of judgement, sternness, and frigidity are transformed into freedom, relaxation, and joy. As Jesus sat at Zacchaeus' table, watching the real Zacchaeus rise from the tomb of alienation and self-deception which he himself had built, Jesus said that salvation had come to that house. For in the workings of the love of God, we have only to declare our lostness to begin the process whereby we are found; we have only to recognize our masks to begin to discern our true face; we have only to realize the deadness of our emotions, our relationships, and our self-esteem to begin in that moment our road to resurrection.

The Samaritan

(Jesus said,) "Which of these...
was neighbour to the man...?" He answered,
"The one who showed him kindness".

Luke 10:36

It was the fashion of those days for a teacher to dispute in public. As with the modern "open line show" on radio, the results were varied. Sometimes dialogue was creative and satisfying, sometimes abrasive and exhausting.

One question from the crowd comes not as a genuine enquiry but as a trap. As such Jesus fences with it, he counters with another question. The incident passes, but only for a moment. Again the voice comes out of the crowd, "Who is my neighbor?" Cynical and threatening in attitude and tone, this question is one which humanity asks in every generation in a hundred ways. "What must I do to inherit eternal life?" "How do I find meaning in life?" "What's the point?"

The response Jesus gives shows the Jewish genius at its best. When asked such a question about the meaning of life, the Greek instinct tends to philosophize and to offer many brilliant insights. The Jewish instinct goes to the heart of the matter with devastating simplicity, often in the form of a story.

The choice of a Samaritan as the central character affirms the recurring Bible warning that God constantly chooses the outsider, the unexpected or forgotten person, the marginal man, to be his agent. The fact that Jesus makes a Samaritan the hero in the drama is in itself enough to rivet the attention of the listeners. For them, as Jesus knows, the Samaritan is an absolute outsider in the most brutal and contemptuous sense. As we listen to the story with this in mind, we hear Jesus pointing out once again the ways in which the rules of the kingdom challenge and sometimes seem to contradict the rules of the world.

The priest and the Levite are, if you will, the professionals. The job, fundamentally, is to help. But in the end help comes from the layman and the non-professional. We forget so easily that this is possible. We are a generation which looks for help only from the professional — the psychiatrist, the doctor, the marriage counsellor, the priest. Only rarely do we enjoy deep relationships with friends which allow us, even when we think of it, to expect help from them in our worry or crisis or agony. But Jesus reminds us that helping and healing are activities not necessarily limited to the professional. He seems to be indicating that there are situations where the professional cannot help, where the only possible assistance must come from another human being having the time, the patience, and the sensitivity to give themselves wholly to the healing of another.

The wounds in our society are beyond number. To respond to them there are a multitude of organizations and systems. Very often, especially in great cities, the part played by these organizations becomes fragmenting and alienating in the lives of those who are to be helped. There will often be many sources of money, many offices and buildings to be trudged to, many forms to be filled out, many social workers to be seen. And what the human being who is the focus of all this is crying for, is a simple, continuing, and trusting relationship with someone who has the time, patience, and concern to stay with the situation.

In the episode of the Samaritan Jesus shows not just an isolated act of kindness, but the infinitely more costly offering of a continuing relationship. Notice how the relationship deepens at various levels. The Samaritan sees the man and then makes the choice to become involved. He tends him with oil and wine. He could at that point have left with a reasonably clear conscience. Instead he takes the problem with him. In the inn he continues to bear responsibility. Then, even at the point of leaving, he opens the door to extending that responsibility after his return.

"Go," said Jesus, "and do thou likewise." If we consider what standard of neighborliness Jesus sends us to, it can have an extremely sobering effect!

The Wind

(Jesus said,) "The wind blows where it wills;
you hear the sound of it, but you do not know
where it comes from, or where it is going."

John 3:8

Nicodemus came to see Jesus by night. People in high places have to be careful. Criticism by our peers can be devastating, and the last thing is to give people the impression that you are letting down the system. When you are highly placed in public life and have everything to lose by making a careless move, you watch yourself very carefully if you wish to survive. But what if you are haunted by something which won't rest until you track it down? Half of you wants to do this and the other half is afraid of real danger. What if this is the situation? For all these reasons Jesus' visitor came by night.

His name was Nicodemus. His assured role and position was at the very top in the national cabinet called the Sanhedrin. Nicodemus was the custodian of a great tradition. He was supposed to be, and expected to be, a national expert on God!

But he had met a stranger — we don't know how — casually passing a group in the temple area, or visiting a house to hear a Rabbi from the north; it could have been thus or otherwise. But Nicodemus had been at first interested in a patronizing way, then intrigued, and finally to his surprise and alarm magnetically drawn. They may have met at the house in Bethany. That's where Jesus often stayed at night when he was down south. That too would be safely away from Jerusalem, from its sentries, and from the community in which Nicodemus usually moved.

For Christians the conversation between Jesus and Nicodemus is one of the great shining jewels of the New Testament. Nicodemus begins by trying to reassure this rural teacher, who might be overawed by such a visitor. Jesus has certain powers; he must then be genuine. It's quite logical. But with devastating directness Jesus dismisses the cool deductions of Nicodemus and speaks of the need to experience the presence of God and offer oneself to him. Nicodemus counters with levity. The Rabbi must be joking with this image of being born again! Surely they are chatting as intelligent men, are they not?

Again Jesus moves in without mercy. Nicodemus has a great deal of information, an endless supply of learning; for him there is a magnificent system of religion in which God is categorized and analyzed. Jesus does not so much say that this is evil or even undesirable; he says rather that it is not enough. There is another level of knowing God. The image which Jesus uses is a tantalizing one. He speaks of a wind, an unpredictable wind which you cannot order at your wish nor predict when it blows. Something deep down in Nicodemus is drawn to what Jesus is saying. Layers of being, beyond thought and analysis and speculation, live within him like ancient instruments not played for many years. And here is a voice plucking at those half forgotten strings of his being, making him a far-off music that is wild and fierce and joyous.

We never see how they part that night. All we do know is that months afterward, when his peers on the Sanhedrin are preparing to move against Jesus, Nicodemus manages to postpone the inevitable clash, not without risk to his position. Still later Nicodemus assists Joseph of Arimathea with the body of the man who had argued him above reason. Nicodemus had become haunted by the distant sound of the wind which Jesus had spoken of. He had begun to suspect that there is more to the relationship between God and his creatures than merely a law, a system, an organization, a formal belonging, a distant acquaintance. Nicodemus had begun to suspect that God is a lover who wishes to possess and be possessed, to be known not merely as information but to be experienced as friend, as Lord, as Saviour.

The Question

When he came to the territory of Caesarea Philippi,
Jesus asked his disciples... "Who do you say I am?"
Matthew 16:13

All of us know what it is to look for affirmation and assurance.
We do it most often when the going is rough. If we receive some
reinforcement of what we are about, we are enabled to keep
going. In a sense, to seek assurance is an admission of weakness
and human need. Sometimes we have great difficulty ascribing
such need to Jesus.

They entered the area of Caesarea Philippi in the process of a
long journey from their familiar surroundings. They had come
west to the coast and then headed north as far as Tyre. Then
they had turned inland again, eastward across the high plateau
north of the lake, until they came to Caesarea Philippi. It was a
foreign place to these men who were used to the towns and the
lakeside. The city had been built by Philip, another generation
of the Herodian family, and it was a garrison town for the
Roman army, full of all the architecture, imagery, and life styles
of Graeco-Roman urban civilization. Sexuality and violence ran
rampant in this centre for the worship of the great god Pan.

Here in this metropolis of power and sophistication, Jesus
turns to his disciples and asks what people are saying about him.
How do they see his work? Who is he in their minds? Probably
taken aback by the question, the disciples dredge their
memories for overheard remarks, snatches of shared conversation, opinions circulating in the fishing towns of the lake area.
Jesus himself is aware of some of this. He knows only too well
the attitude of his own town of Nazareth, and the memory probably hurts.

The replies of the disciples are varied, as are those of each of us
today when Jesus, through someone else's lips, asks us the same
question, and with increasing frequency and intensity. Who do
you say I am? So simple a question in its words but so profound
in its implications. It comes in many guises. We are singing a
hymn or saying the creed, and suddenly the question comes,
"What do I really believe about this?" We are having one of
those casual conversations which make it possible to get

through some social situations, and somehow we have stumbled into an area which involves faith or church. Does one play along or quickly communicate one's stance of faith? In such moments and in many others we find ourselves in unexpected "Caesarea Philippi" encounters.

The disciples list a whole series of labels that people have applied to Jesus. And these names reveal all the different expectations held about him. Some thought of him as an Elijah, working toward a real confrontation with the powers that be. Would Jesus do that? Some saw him more like Jeremiah, no less vehement but concentrating more on the inner journey, the private side of life.

It is fascinating that these images are still struggling among his disciples today. Some say the individual Christian and the church should be Elijah figures, confronting systems, institutions, national policies. That was the way Elijah saw his task. Look at the First Book of Kings in the Old Testament (Chapters 17 to 21). Some say, like Jeremiah, that the domain of Christ, through his church, is the personal and private side of life. Significantly Jesus probes beyond both and asks, "You, who do you say I am." In Peter's answer, "You are Messiah," blurted out with his typical impetuosity, we are given a concept that involves both of the above ideas and goes beyond them. The Messiah came into society, and into individual lives, in a total way, reconciling the distinctions between public and private.

Above all, this question asked of the disciples echoes through time as the classic point of decision for every Christian. The church has much to teach about Jesus Christ from its long tradition, and obviously we can learn from that. We can experience the love of Christ in the community of the church, and indeed beyond that community we can discover his love in places and circumstances where he is not even named. But everyone has at some stage got to come to Caesarea Philippi and answer the question, "You, who do you say I am?"

The Search for Power

James and John... approached him and said,...
"Grant us the right to sit in state with you"...
Jesus said to them, "You do not understand
what you are asking."

Mark 10:35

It is significant that on this occasion Peter was not included, because so often events included Peter and James and John. This time the two brothers acted on their own in a way that one can only assume arose not so much from crass selfishness as from a total misreading of all that Jesus was trying to teach them. Mark says that James and John came to Jesus and asked that they be given the chief seats in the kingdom which they understood to be coming. Matthew recalls the incident a little differently. In his narrative it is the mother of the two brothers who approaches Jesus with them, and she asks the favour.

We are dealing here with simple men and women (simple does not mean stupid) by whom vast and complex religious concepts are seen in very clearly defined images. The Messiah will come, the tradition had told them, and when he comes he will usher in a kingdom. It will be a time of joy and triumph and celebration, a time of peace and plenty and justice.

But under the lilting melody of that Jewish vision of a messianic kingdom, there was a deep and terrible music. It had been sounded by that long dead and unknown genius we call Isaiah, who had sung the songs of the Servant of God who would suffer. For the kingdom, like all kingdoms, comes at a great cost. This is what the two otherwise loving and loyal friends had forgotten, if indeed they had ever understood it. Jesus realizes this. His whole attitude is one not of contempt but of disappointed and understanding affection. He carefully reminds James and John of the cost and asks if they can pay it. With the eternal and enviable confidence of youth they assure him they can. He accepts, even though he knows that they have no idea of the terrible "baptism" which awaits their hopes and dreams.

We ask James and John's question today in many ways. As Christians in Western society we have had the "chief places" for a long time, for about sixteen centuries. As Christians we have reflected and made sacred the power structures of our society. This is not necessarily evil. To some extent religion must always play a consolidating and validating role in society. But that role has to be mixed with the role of critic and prophet. The mixing is not easy but it is essential.

Sometimes many of us wish for that kind of long ago kingdom to come again — the voice of the church relevant in high places, theology sought after by other disciplines as a modern resource, and much else. Yet the Christ of this century offers us something more costly — the task of creating Christian community within and around the traditional church and its structures, the working out of theology which offers insights about today's issues, the discovery of worship forms which make it possible to celebrate life as God's gift in the midst of a very challenging age.

There are other ways we echo that request of James and John without realizing it. There is a type of Christian enthusiasm prevalant today which understands a relationship with God only in terms of the joy and health, the energy and success which life brings. The blessing of God is seen in terms of the presence of a kingdom given now. Again, while this is not evil, it is incomplete. The presence of God is not always in terms only of human happiness or enthusiasm or even, if we can dare to say it, in loyalty and faith. C. S. Lewis is associated more than anything else with his use of the word *joy*. It is interesting that he used it, not so much to describe his sense of the abiding presence of God as to speak of the ongoing longing for God, a longing which he experienced in both intimate nearness and beckoning distance.

When Jesus had dealt gently with James and John, he went on to speak of the issue behind their request. He spoke of power and servanthood. He pointed out that what the brothers had asked for was power and authority, the universal human temptation. He reminded them that the whole point of his own life was to revolutionize power by showing that true power is servanthood. We do not serve God merely in our power — our health, success, attractiveness, or leadership qualities. We also serve him in our weakness, in our struggles to find him, in our feelings of inadequacy or loneliness or guilt. God is not present in our times of power, and absent in our times of weakness. In both he is always our God and our Father.

Lost and Found

*"My boy," said the father... How could we help
celebrating..." "Your brother here was dead
and has come back to life, was lost and is found."*

Luke 15:32

The story in which something is lost, searched for and found is
universal and timeless. We tell it to children, we tell it in
endless versions in novels, films, and television. It doesn't seem
to matter what it is that is lost. Sometimes it will be a ring, as in
Tolkien's great saga, *The Lord of the Rings*; sometimes it will be
a lost world, a lost city, a lost continent. What seems to matter
is that someone, alone or with others, sets out on a search for it
and finds it. There is always a reason why such stories become
universal. There must be a deep need in the human psyche to
which they speak. If we tell the story of something lost being
searched for and found, then the odds are that at the heart of
human experience there is a "lost" quality.

Many have tried to express that lost quality, to put words to
what is lost. Two who come to mind are the poet Wordsworth
who wrote "Intimations of Immortality from Recollections of
Early Childhood," and C. S. Lewis who wrote *Surprised by Joy*.
Each in his own way is describing an experience which we have
all shared, that of sensing in our deepest being a reality, a com-
pleteness, a peace, a kingdom of which we get fragmentary
glimpses in our lives. Much as one would wish to, we cannot
make the experience last; we cannot live in the discovered
kingdom. Lewis particularly spoke of our day-to-day lives as
being lived in a kind of exile from another country. From time to
time we are allowed to make brief unplanned visits to it, but
never to stay while we have other tasks to complete in our exile.

Jesus used this theme in his efforts to tell men and women of
what he called his kingdom, and Luke gathers the images
together. There is the shepherd who has lost the sheep, the
woman who has lost a silver piece, the father who has lost a son.
In each story Jesus tells of the one who becomes lost, of those
who search and find, and then of the rejoicing which follows. All
three are in effect the same story. In all three Jesus is saying that
the kingdom comes for us when we find what we have lost.

But what is this kingdom, this being lost and being found, or this losing and finding? For the Christian that answer has to be sought on many levels. In the dawn of the world a man tried to express that "lostness" in his story of the garden which was given to, and lost by, man and woman. In our own journey we speak of "losing our way" or of "finding ourselves." We speak of "losing touch" with one another or of "finding God."

Perhaps the first step in our discovery of what Jesus meant by the kingdom, is to realize that he is talking about all of our human experiences, not just what we and our compartmentalized world call our religious experience. In all our experience there is an incompleteness or lostness. Something is missing which we long for. Even in our deepest human relationships there are things lost or missing. In everything we achieve or build or create there is the same tantalizing missing element. Yet scattered throughout all our experiences there are moments when we seem to break through into what that experience could be at its ultimate depth and height. Humdrum emotions discover a lost ecstasy. Ordinary relationships discover a lost intimacy. Everyday scenes take on a lost beauty. Familiar words assume a lost significance. Familiar symbols assume a lost power to move and to inspire. What is merely the setting sun of other evenings becomes on this particular evening the vestibule of heaven. What is merely the wine of other Sundays becomes this Sunday both terror and sweetness, the blood of God.

In such moments, undeserving and unexpecting, we stumble upon the door to the kingdom and receive sufficient of its glory to enable us to live until the door again opens.

> O world invisible, we view thee,
> O world intangible, we touch thee,
> O world unknowable, we know thee,
> Inapprehensible, we clutch thee!
>
> The angels keep their ancient places; —
> Turn but a stone, and start a wing!
> 'Tis ye, 'tis your estranged faces,
> That miss the many-splendoured thing.
>
> "In No Strange Land" —
> Francis Thompson

The Sower

(Jesus said,) A sower went out to sow. And as he sowed, some seed fell along the footpath... on rocky ground... among thistles... into good soil.

Matthew 13:4

In the years between Jesus' ministry and the writing of the first gospel, people told and re-told many remembered things. There were words he had said, incidents and encounters of all kinds, stories he had told. Among them were the stories of the kingdom. As we know, Jesus often described the kingdom in terms of the "lost and the found." He seemed to suggest that when we find ourselves, or find areas of ourselves which seemed lost or broken or forgotten, then we stumble into the kingdom of God, because it is he who really does the finding, sometimes through the love, patience, and sensitivity of another human being.

Another image which he used very often is that of seed being sown. His followers remembered how, when speaking of the kingdom, he would sometimes glance around for something to use as an illustration. He might point across to the other side of one of the valleys of Galilee. There a man would be walking up and down a field, a familiar puff of dust floating away from him as he threw the seed in front and to each side, while behind him a flock of birds wheeled, circled, and cried their greed and excitement.

The best known story Jesus ever told using the image of the seed is, of course, that of the sower. To his listeners this was something totally familiar. Off went the seed in every direction, and this is a significant element in the story. Jesus is always painting a portrait of the Father. The image in this story is that of the prodigality of God. Thorns choke the seed, birds swoop and devour it, rocks bake it dry, yet the sower just continues to throw it out in all directions! Jesus is pointing the way in which God fills every aspect of life with signs of his presence. It would appear that God is extremely unselective where he drops these innumerable hints, signs, or seeds of himself. How often we are told what happens to the seed — the devil comes and carries it off, it dies from lack of roots, it is "choked by cares and wealth and the pleasures of life," yet how seldom it is emphasized that God goes on and on throwing it in every possible direction.

The other truth deep in this story of the sower is the extent to which Christian life is so much an ongoing process rather than a single, climactic event. The seed falls and is taken by a whole cross-section of human types in many situations. The acid test is not the gobbling up of the seed but the growing of it. There are many who think that Jesus' answer to the question of his disciples (Luke 8:9), in which he explains the story he has just told, is actually a piece of teaching from an early Christian sermon. For in no other instance does Jesus explain a parable. This surmise is interesting but not important. Jesus' concluding words about "the seed in good soil" are describing a life-long process. This is important!

Recall that all this story-telling is Jesus' way of describing the kingdom of God. Our Lord seems to be saying that the possession of the kingdom in a human life is a process not only of discovering God (the seed), but also of offering one's self as a person (piece of ground), in which there begins deepening, nourishing, growing, maturing, on and on through many seasons of response (harvest). There is a most beautiful and ancient word for this process. It is called sanctification, growth in holiness; and when we see it in a human life, it attracts us by its beauty, its dependability, and its capacity to radiate the love and goodness of God.

Our Lord presents Christian living as an on-going process rather than a single event. At present there is a tendency to express excitement and joy about the moment in which a person discovers Christ and finds himself called to respond to him. That moment, as we know, is called *conversion*. Our time is rich in opportunities for conversion. The turmoil and change, the capacity of today's world to probe deeply into our fears and anxieties — these things bring many to a new discovery of the reality of Jesus as ultimately full of meaning for them. That is good and wonderful, but the test is in the transition from the experience of that conversion to the lifelong process of sanctification. Jesus used shorter words to say that. "The seed... (in) good soil," he said, is the man who hears the word and understands it, who accordingly bears fruit... (Matthew 13:23).

The Seed

> *(Jesus said,) "The kingdom of Heaven is like*
> *a mustard-seed... it becomes a tree."*
>
> Matthew 13:31

"The kingdom of God is like..." Jesus would say, and the image chosen would always be something familiar seen in a new way.

Today you drive up Mount Tabor by taxi. The road goes south from Nazareth and then turns left, or east. Soon you begin twisting and turning up the steep narrow mountain road until you emerge in front of the church and community house which today crown Tabor. From there you can see most of Galilee below and all around you. And if you are fortunate (or if you ask), the priest on duty will take you to a spot in the lovely gardens and put into your hands some tiny black seeds.

They are mustard seeds. These are the seeds which Jesus must often have run through his fingers as he moved across the countryside. One day he thought of them as he spoke again about the kingdom of God, and pointed to the tree that grows from these tiny seeds. The kingdom too is something that grows from a tiny beginning. In all his statements about the kingdom of God, Jesus is describing the way in which the Father works. God, Jesus implies, likes to do things by growing them.

Take, for example, words and concepts such as holiness and spirituality. They are rather frightening words. One tends to think of special names, great figures from scripture and history, and say that they were holy; that they possessed deep spirituality. But in a sense we are wrong on both counts. It would be more correct to say that they *became* holy, that they entered a deep spirituality. Holiness and spirituality are not ready-made and complete states of being. It is not that X is holy and Y is not, that X is spiritual and Y is not. The truth is that we must choose to take the early steps on the journey which leads to holiness. And what does holiness mean? Perhaps more than anything else it means a conscious effort to mirror in one's living the nature of God as one knows him and has seen him in Jesus.

There are a few very important things here. One is that I must choose to begin that journey. The instant I do so, I have achieved a spirituality. Spirituality is not a state arrived at down the line.

The day I begin even to long to do the will of God, I have emerged into spirituality. It may be an early spirituality, a ''seed spirituality,'' but it has begun.

The second important thing is that to choose the spiritual way is not to become less than who I am. The only things in life which have to diminish, or even die, are things which will never be worthy of God's consecration. But all our gifts are initially acceptable, totally varied though they may be. We are often impressed by lives that express a new relationship with God by totally changing their direction. The more drastic the change, the more impressive appears the degree of spiritual decision and discovery. The prima ballerina becomes a sister with some missionary order, the gangster becomes a social worker, the pornographer becomes a preacher. But comparatively few people have exotic occupations such as that of ballerina, gangster, or pornographer. For most of us the spiritual journey begins when we offer what we already are doing as a gift to God, asking him to accept us and use us as who and what we are.

Look at the seed in Jesus' hand as he speaks. It is tiny, simple, unimpressive. Yet he says that the kingdom of God is like that. With us the beginning of the kingdom may well be like that too. It is far more likely to begin in simple ways than in the dramatic. We hear of the dramatic change, the sudden conversion, only because they are the stepping out of the norm which is the experience of most people. For most people the road to holiness, the first step in spirituality, is often a deceptively simple decision — to pick up an article or book to read, to be haunted by some image seen or some word heard, to accept an invitation to go to a particular group or meeting — the list is endless. But each of these possibilities is the tiny seed from which grows the tree of faith, the tree of spirituality. ''The kingdom of God,'' said Jesus, ''What shall I compare it with? It is like a mustard seed... It grew to be a tree...''

The Enemy

(Jesus said,) "The kingdom of Heaven is like this.
A man sowed his field with good seed; but...
his enemy came, (and) sowed darnel among the wheat."
Matthew 13:24

More than anyone else Matthew seems fascinated by Jesus' use of the seed as a way of speaking about the kingdom of God. He alone relates a story which has a great deal to say about the realism of Jesus' thinking.

Jesus has again turned to the fields for his image. In those fields of Galilee grew most of the corn on which the rest of the country depended. But it was particularly vulnerable to a certain weed which the *New English Bible* calls "darnel." This weed was dreaded because in the early stages of growth it is almost indistinguishable from the young corn. In Jesus' story an enemy sows darnel in a man's cornfield. Servants, seeing it and anxious to root it out, ask if they can go to work. The owner stops them on the grounds that weeding the field now will destroy the crop as well. Leave it to the harvest, is his opinion, because that is the best time for distinguishing the weed from good crop.

We are now hearing from Jesus a more ominous note about the kingdom. The kingdom of heaven is not a sunlit fairyland; it is more a battleground. There is an enemy, not clumsy, ineffective, and easily dealt with, but subtle, intelligent, elusive, and therefore formidable. All through the Bible sincere respect is always paid to the power of evil. It is never dismissed as irrelevant, never treated casually. It is never forgotten that the evil one is essentially an angel, albeit a fallen angel; therefore his powers are formidable. The devil with whom Jesus wrestles in the wilderness is an adversary not easily overcome. Indeed it is significant that far from being overcome he departs only temporarily. Luke is the writer who uses the most threatening phrase. At the end of his description of the wilderness struggle, he writes that "the devil departed, biding his time."

Milton continues that attitude of utter realism towards evil in his portrait of Satan in "Paradise Lost." Satan has about him a dark magnificence which bodes ill for those who do not take him seriously. A final and very modern image which gives us the same warning, is the huge metal sculpture on the wall of Coventry Cathedral showing Michael the Archangel standing over a half-recumbent Satan. Each great angel, that of light and that of darkness, is massive and powerful. Although Satan is down, he is not totally subdued but threatens to rise again.

This acknowledgement of the power of evil is in Jesus' parable. The coming of the kingdom, whether in terms of a person's life or in the forms and institutions of a society, is not an easy process, nor in terms of time and history is it ever a guaranteed process. Always there is the inevitable struggle with forces that would destroy the growing seed. Jesus tells of the servants' longing for a crop free from weed, for the perfect cornfield. We all share this longing in our world. We long for a personality free from the weeds of anxiety, fear, and depression. We long for a church free from the weeds of apathy and helplessness. We long for a society free from the weeds of injustice, pollution, war, and resource depletion.

In the face of these longings our Lord is almost brutally realistic. Within time and history our longings will never be satisfied. But they are legitimate. The hope which they represent is absolutely essential to human life. If we lost the dream which all those longings represent, we would disintegrate under depression and hopelessness. But our Lord points out that, while time and history last, every single aspect of life will be full of the ambiguities which we long to resolve. There will never be a complete resolution of the personal struggles within me and my relationships. But I must always strive for personal peace and growth and maturity. There will never be a complete resolution of the ambiguities of society. But I must go on trying to live and act and contribute towards their partial resolution. There will never be a full resolution of all that prevents me from entering into a complete intimacy with God and the spiritual things of God. But I must continue my journey into the high places where he dwells.

Hope lives in the owner's reply to the servants. Harvest is the time for separating the corn from the weed. There will be a resolution of life's ambiguities. There will be an end of the partial, and a discovery and tasting of the complete, the whole. But the time of the harvest is God's time.

The Hiding Place

The kingdom of Heaven is like treasure lying buried in a field. The man who found it... sold everything he had, and bought that field.

Matthew 13:44

Jesus never ceased seeking images to help people understand what he meant by his expression, "the kingdom." Sometimes he used the idea of something hidden. As with the other images, this one came out of the fabric of everyday life. The kingdom, Jesus would suggest, is like a woman baking a cake and putting into it a little yeast. That little bit of yeast affects the whole cake. Again, the kingdom is like a treasure hidden in a field. Someone becomes aware of it and buys the field. Or it is like a costly pearl which turns up in a caravan cargo. The person who knows its value snaps it up even if he has to sell everything else to get it.

God, Jesus seems to be saying, acts in a hidden way. Jesus himself is a living instance of this. The eyes of a civilization seeking for power, creativity, and change are all fixed on Rome. Yet it is away from that focus where God acts. Rome is not the divine centre; it is Bethlehem. Jewish tradition looks to a Messiah who will come with power and charisma to conquer. But there comes a village carpenter. Instead of seeking his following in the centre of power, at Jerusalem, he remains secluded in the hills of Galilee. Instead of outlining a political plan, he speaks of a kingdom concealed in the human heart and in the designs of God. When finally he submits to the terrible wheel of history which revolves to crush him, he lies sheltered in the tomb and then emerges as conquerer of death.

When the very early Christians still regarded the Old Testament as their only scripture, they thought of God entering human affairs in a hidden way. They would look at the story of Joseph, who is sent off to Egypt by his brothers and remains there unknown to them until they go to Egypt for corn. Even then he remains hidden until he tells them who he is. Again the early Christians looked at the old story of Jonah. Here was God's agent sent to do his will. For three days he enters into the belly of the whale. It matters not in the least whether we wish to take the story literally or not. It is the hiddenness that matters, the fact that God carries out his will in unexpected ways.

In these parables, Jesus is drawing on his own rich Jewish background. All through the Bible God slips into human experience in disguises. For Moses it is by way of a bush burning in his everyday landscape. For Hosea it is by the pain and loneliness of his tragic marriage. If this is indeed the way God works, then it is absolutely essential that we cultivate the gift of being aware of such possibilities. Then, whenever we do stumble on the presence and activity of God in situations, we will be ready to respond. In the stories of the hiddenness of the kingdom, the picture is always that of a person hard at work and actively looking. They are aware that there may be treasure under that grubby earth, that there may be in the pile of mediocre jewelry a real diamond. And when the treasure is turned up by the spade or plough, when the diamond drops out on the table, they are ready and willing to act. Notice how they act. Both men in the stories (Matthew 13:44) sold everything they had. What is offered and what has been discovered has a price tag. Other things may have to be jettisoned to get the one priceless thing.

If indeed God works this way, then we are wise always to presume the possibility of his activity in places that are hidden. If we regard an area of life as ordinary and everyday and pedestrian, then let us beware! Bushes burn in ordinary, pedestrian, dusty deserts! If we come to take some relationships for granted, then let us be careful! Under ordinary fields there may be treasure. If colleagues at work, or the place itself, or its tasks, have begun to feel soul-destroying, it is just possible that somewhere hidden in that situation is an element which can become an entry point into new possibilities, and a door into the kingdom.

Palms and Hosannas

(Jesus said,) "Go to the village opposite; ...you will find tethered there a colt... If anyone asks why you are untying it, say, "Our Master needs it."

Luke 19:30

On a visit to Israel today you can take a taxi or tour bus about half-way up the road that winds south-east over the Mount of Olives. In front of you the slope drops away to the Kidron Valley. From there it climbs up again to the walls of the old city lying across your vision from left to right. You can see the gates which are set in those walls, some still used and some closed up.

Near where you are standing Jesus once stood. The view he saw was in the main what you see, the hill and the valley and the city. What is missing for you, and what must have been over-whelmingly significant for Jesus, was Herod's temple, then one of the most magnificent buildings in the whole Mediterranean world. Six city blocks long, its battlements at their pinnacle reaching to 120 feet, the sanctuary itself higher than a Gothic cathedral, the whole shining snow white in the blazing sun — the temple represented power, establishment, system, order, authority. We do not know what went through Jesus' mind as he stood near this spot and looked at that city and that temple. But we do know that he saw this great and ancient tradition as having lost the vision of his Father's love within a vast, complex, politicized religious system. That thought filled Jesus with almost inexpressible sadness.

By the time Jesus stood here, at the beginning of the last week of his life, he had come to believe that somehow, not only that system but all the many systems which manipulated and ordered human life at that time, were killing the capacity of people to reach for God's kingdom. He realized by now that such systems had to be challenged even if this meant the ultimate cost to himself.

On this hillside the drama we know so well began. He sent the disciples to get him an animal. It was not a noble animal, giving a semblance of power and dignity to the rider as in the Roman triumphal processions. Yet in these circumstances Jesus chose a recognized symbol of potential power. The memory of the words spoken by the prophet Zechariah had been imprinted on every Jewish mind many years before. He had foretold that Zion's king would come riding upon an ass. Jesus knew well that he had only to mount this animal and move forward down the slope to openly declare himself more than a Rabbi and more than a teacher.

As the Lord Christ moves through the inner country of the human soul, he steadily shows himself to be more than when we first encounter him. He approaches first as childhood word, then as youthful question, perhaps later as adulthood's fading memory. Then we may experience him returning to our consciousness, seeking renewed acquaintance, later on asking for serious consideration, eventually demanding our obedience, loyalty, and finally our worship.

When Jesus approaches that long ago city, the thunder of acclamation swells. But deeper and distant, at other levels of the city's life, the thunder of rejection and retribution gathers. So it is when the Lord tries to move against the walls and gates of our own inner city, that city which we hold so jealously against any invasion, where even familiar friends are allowed only with care, and then only into areas prepared and selected for their presence. We offer both welcome and warning, acceptance and distrust.

Yet Jesus entered Jerusalem that day, and he enters the human heart day-by-day until time ends. To each he offers a kingdom, a way of experiencing life, an intimacy with himself. To each he comes gently, forcing nothing more than a choice which must be made about him, to welcome or reject, to acknowledge a king or to repel an intruder. It is so easy to forget that in every Eucharist we cry out the choice that we have made. We say, "Blessed is he that cometh in the name of the Lord. Hosanna in the highest." Do these words really reflect the decision we have made or are they just familiar words in a familiar liturgy?

The Challenge

When he came in sight of the city he wept over it and said, "If only you had known on this great day, the way that leads to peace!"

Luke 19:41

Human beings build systems. We build them usually for good reason and with the very best intentions. To help each other keep healthy we build a medical system. To exchange the fruits, the grain, or the metals of the earth, we build a trade system. To worship, pray, search for God, we build a religious system. All this is both good and bad, because our intentions are good but the result is often tragic.

Look around the temple in Jerusalem as Jesus saw it. The vast stone platform on which it stands is alive with people from every corner of the earth. Believers, scattered over the known world, look to this spot as being truly the place of God's dwelling. They support the temple's life with a yearly tax payment. Into this building there pours an avalanche of money, bringing with it choices, responsibilities, political intrigues, the temptations of power. The original purpose of this great complex machinery which throbs around Jesus was once simple. At heart, in its best moments and in its best people, it is still simple. It is searching for and mediating God to his sons and daughters. But the nature of systems is to forget their origins.

Not long ago I was walking around St Peter's great Basilica in Rome. It dwarfs one's humanity. It communicates on a vast scale. One moves in a great history, looks at great art. Suddenly I passed a side chapel and saw what was obviously a family and a few friends gathered around a priest who was in the act of baptising a baby. In that moment I felt a wholeness created for me, a bond made which I had thought broken between grandeur and humility, between history and human life, between crowds and the individual, between complexity and simplicity. It came as a reassurance that a great system had not become divorced from the essential simplicity which constituted His heart and soul.

Yet for Jesus there came no such scene and no such reassurance. The thriving industry around him dominated everything else. A hundred currencies came here from across the world and had to be exchanged in order to purchase sacrificial birds or animals. Perhaps Jesus recalled Joseph telling him as a child how he had bought the cheapest sacrifice possible when he and Mary had taken their child to this same temple.

Suddenly Jesus moved, swiftly and purposefully. We will never know to what extent the act was spontaneous or calculated. He heaved up a table laden with coins; he went from there to a stall of chirping birds, overturning, gesticulating, shouting. We will never know how the episode ended, whether he was stopped by anxious friends, or whether the attack was so sudden and unthinkable in that particular place that he was gone before response was possible.

We live and work and organize our lives in an infinite number of ways — educational, sociological, religious, economic, technological, and many more. Until recently we took most of these for granted in their present forms. They operated without serious question, without change or challenge. But that is no longer true. In all their temples we hear tables being rudely overturned; devastating questions being asked. Are schools on the wrong track? Is the church capable of enabling the search for God in human lives? Are classical capitalism, communism, and socialism working any more? On and on the questions go.

The greatest question perhaps is this — Who is asking the questions? Whose is the hand overturning the tables in the great "temples" of the contemporary world? Is it only political enemies, radicals, iconoclasts, terrorists? Or could it be one who walks among us with total justice and utter love, who will not allow our carefully constructed systems to continue without challenge?

Conflict

Jesus said, "In very truth I tell you, before Abraham was born, I am." They picked up stones to throw at him, but Jesus was not to be seen; and he left the temple.

John 8:58

There is a rhythm about this terrible week. It swings between day and night, city and countryside, enmity and friendship, pressure and relaxation. There is never a time when we see Jesus more human than during these days, never a time when we can more easily identify with him as he moves between the familiar polarities of life. We know a great deal about these last few days. Each of the evangelists shows us events in detail. Vague continuity phrases such as "soon after" or "about that time" or "it came to pass" are gone from the gospel narrative. Almost each hour is accounted for, as they relate the ultimate tragedy, scene by vivid scene, act by terrifying act.

Each of these days was spent in the city, particularly in its heart which was the temple area, the centre of everything — finance, education, socializing, public debate. To this centre the crowds gathered like magic; from it news travelled with the speed of wild fire. Each morning Jesus came over the Mount of Olives road, in through one of the gates, and up one of the great wide staircases which led to the courtyards, the bazaars, the debating places, the rabbinical schools, the sanctuary itself. All during this day he presented his case. On many occasions he had used a mysterious phrase. At the long ago happy occasion of the wedding of Cana he had said to his mother, "My hour has not yet come." Now, standing in the shadow of a pillar, looking out across the sun-drenched stones of the temple courtyards, fielding questions from friends and enemies, he seems to have decided that the hour had come. The entrenched systems which dominated the lives of his people and time had to be challenged. The challenge came in the name of "the kingdom of God."

Sometimes we know in our spiritual journey that an hour has come when a word has to be said, a position stated, an allegiance revealed, even though the word may be rejected, the position challenged, the allegiance ridiculed. Such hours come in personal lives and in the life of institutions. Sometimes the church must ask unwelcome questions about the systems around it, asking in the name of the kingdom of God, even if the questions are dismissed as utopian, naive, unrealistic. Tension brings exhaustion. We see our Lord taste the exhaustion that we sometimes know — the tension of being on guard among others, of wondering who can be trusted and who cannot, the heart-break of offering utterly and being rejected, the mental drain of endless argument. When we take all this to him in mumbled and desperate prayer, we take it to One who knows it in his own experience.

At sundown when the crowds drift away and the heat lessens, there are a few friends left, and plans are made to go to a house for a glass of wine. It could be the house of Mary and her son John Mark, or one of the many houses where another wine would soon be drunk, the story of his agony and triumph recited, and the cup lifted and passed. But this is not yet come. Now he reaches for his cloak and prepares to leave the city for the night. The streets are empty and darkening; on the temple wall the sentries of the Herodian guard are silhouetted against the evening sky. He gets to the city gate before it closes for the night and heads into the darkening east. It's a good hour to Bethany, down the slope and over the Kidron brook, up through the wooded slopes of the Mount of Olives, along the road among the trees, and soon home.

At the end of the road are friends, familiar trusted faces, tenderness, welcome, nourishment, love. In the hours of this week we see God at his most human, the divine self-emptying at its most sublime. He who is ultimate love needs love himself, he who carries within him the inspiration for all human friend-ship needs friendship himself. These moments tell us how freely and fully we can confess our humanity and dependence to him as Lord, knowing that he has himself experienced our frailty as man.

Friends

While they were on their way Jesus came to a village
where a woman named Martha made him welcome...
She had a sister Mary.

Luke 10:38

If the events of Holy Week were staged as a play, the first four days could almost be presented on a set divided down the centre, on one side a public area and on the other the interior of a home at the time. The public area is part of the temple complex in Jerusalem, the home is that of two sisters and a brother — Mary, Martha and Lazarus — in the village of Bethany a few miles east of the city. A public place and a private place — we know them both so well. They represent the almost universal setting of our own lives. The claims of each have to be dealt with, and we rarely find a completely satisfying balance. Home and office, family and colleagues we desperately need, but we resent having to adjust our senses of love and duty to them. Each crushes and recreates us. Each can be the place of love and hatred, loyalty and betrayal. Each can become a refuge from the other.

So it was for Jesus. There are indications that the temple area, in fact the city itself, was a magnet for him and yet a place to be dreaded. Jerusalem and Galilee were poles apart in almost everything. The dry, brown desert wadis of Judea, the blazing sun of the Jordan Valley, the sternness and conservatism of the life style — all contrasted with the openness of Galilee — the rolling wooded hills with green pastures, the shimmering lake, the intimacy of its little towns, the openness of its people. Jerusalem as a concept, as an idea, was probably intriguing and even inspiring to Jesus as a Jew, but also a place of pressure and mistrust for him as a public figure. To our knowledge he never spent a night in the city if he could avoid it, but made the house in Bethany his place of escape. Perhaps in the week of his death he spent a precious day gathering his energy in this quiet spot, sheltered from even the sight of the city by the slope and crown of the Mount of Olives.

He had first discovered this place and these three people as he came to the city from another feast months if not years before. He had, like many other travellers, been exhausted after days of travelling south through the Jordan Valley, resting in Jericho, then beginning the long climb up to Jerusalem from the eastern side. With typical sensitivity Luke tells us about their first discovery of each other and the beginning of that firm friendship. Luke who recalls the vivid contrast between the two women and gives us Jesus' comment to Martha about her busyness.

Mary and Martha stand forever as symbols of the two modes of life between which we continually oscillate. There is no value judgement made on either. It is not that Martha's activity is bad and Mary's contemplative stance is good. Some people regard contemplation as effortless and even uncreative. Nothing could be further from the truth. Activity can become a shield against facing issues and questions and truths which must be allowed to surface if we are to survive. But there are times when we simply must contemplate, must step back, must think, if we are to be capable of returning to activity. Mary and Martha symbolize not so much opposites as necessary facets in any balanced life.

There was another occasion when Jesus arrived at his house having climbed the same road from the valley far below. It was a day of desolation and strongly expressed grief. On that day the door between the worlds opened, and he who stood in that terrifying door between humanity and divinity called to a dead Lazarus, until death bowed its head before the Lord and surrendered its prisoner.

Here in this place Jesus rested. Here he was attended and cared for and loved. No theological disputations took place, no questions were asked to trap him, no ears were listening to gather evidence to harm him. All his life he knew when to withdraw, when frayed nerves simply had to be rested, when energy was depleted. So often we show a kind of pride which refuses to acknowledge this. Yet in this little village, in the home of his dearest friends, the Lord of life makes no secret of weariness or of the need for rest and recuperation. He who taught us to ask without apology for "daily bread" bids us likewise without apology acknowledge our humanity and its limitations and its needs.

The Supper

(Jesus said) "Give this message... The Master says 'Where is the room reserved for me...?' He will show you a large room upstairs, set out in readiness."

Mark 14:14

There is now so little time left. He probably has a feeling that the trap will close at any moment, and yet everything is so incomplete in any human sense. Only thirty-six short months ago he was desperately trying to see his way, in those solitary weeks in the desert after the baptismal commitment and the self discovery. The community has come into being, deepening and maturing, until now these familiar faces and voices mean everything to him and he to them. They are committed, but the mystery still remains, committed to what? Is there a way ahead, a program, a plan? Not really. He himself gives us no hint that he possesses any grand plan. The intimacy with the Father, seeking for the kingdom — these he sees being passed on, spreading even beyond Israel, but there is no explanation of how it is to happen.

With only twenty-four hours left he asks that a room be rented and a meal prepared. On this occasion much is said that we will never know. But three things are done which we see in vivid detail. He takes a towel and water and acts out the role of the lowest servant. And later he takes the familiar wine and bread at the table and shares it. We are given a play, not any hurriedly written book of philosophy or memoirs. There isn't the time, and even if there were, that is not his way. For many, many years the way has been the written word given by the Father in the ancient scrolls. Now it is the living word of his own flesh. He acts out a play, and so reminds us of the eternal Jewish insight and gift to the world — that God himself is Actor and not just Author of the cosmic play. He makes the play from his own acts.

He takes the bread and names it his body; the wine he names his blood. As they share it, they realize that they are no longer twelve individuals. They are becoming a body. For three years the body which is the vehicle of the divine will has been him who sits at the centre of the table. But this is about to end. That body is about to be brutalized by men. But the iron and the leather and the thorns and the cross piece of wood will come too late. The body which has faithfully served the divine purpose will have already passed. For divinity is now at the table passing into the bodies of the disciples, who silently break off the pieces of flat bread and nervously swallow the local red wine.

One does not suggest that they knew all this. Certainly they did not in any formed or conscious way. The process was wiser and more effective than mere explanation and analysis and planning. These are the methods that we are so fond of in our different culture and distant century. In accepting the unspoken invitation to be actors in the play, they felt its power and they knew its purpose — binding them to him indissolubly and yet allowing them absolute freedom.

The acting out of the play did not involve magical effects. The eating and drinking did not make them supermen, did not remove their humanity, nor make them any less vulnerable. The power of the play made them his own. And after the days and weeks ahead, when they would show their most pitiable imitations in fear, cowardice, betrayal, confusion, indecision, and much else — after all that they would still be his and would remain so, and their faithfulness would change history.

The familiar building which we call a church is really the theatre of this eternal play. The narthex is a porch, a foyer for our anticipation. The prayer book is our script. The actors? The actors are only in part those who are costumed for the play. In wearing our normal clothes in the pews we are all costumed, as long ago they came in their Galilean clothes to the room and to the table. We, as they, are the actors, and in our eating of the bread and the drinking of the wine we become as they did — his own. *Deo Gratias!*

The Garden

The third time he came and said to them,
"Still sleeping! Still taking your ease! Enough!
The hour has come."

Mark 14:41

Long after the tension of the final weeks they would remember certain events, certain words, certain feelings and places. At the time they may not have recognized their significance, or they may not have had the opportunity or even the energy to think them through. For three of them there would always remain deep feelings of inadequacy and self-condemnation about those midnight and early morning hours before the last terrible day.

After the supper they had left the room, moved carefully through the streets to the east wall, and then slipped into the shadow of the Kidron Valley. Once there he did something which had occurred a few times before. He asked them to remain where they were. Long afterwards they would wonder whether he had done it for their protection. He then asked Peter and James and John to accompany him. Together they moved up the slopes of the great public garden and were lost among the black pools of shadow thrown by the ancient olive trees. Even at that point they were exhausted. They had undergone long hours in the Upper Room listening to him, sensing the driving urgency in his words, trying desperately to understand what he was telling them, aware of intense emotion vibrating in every word spoken, every glance exchanged, every action carried out. They had moved almost beyond words and certainly beyond any attempts at coherent planning or action. Blindly they followed him into the recesses of the garden.

They had never seen him in the grip of fear before, and it must have severely startled them. Even he was beyond the wish for human community. He groped forward for solitary communion with the Father, telling them to stay where they were. For a while they could hear him. They listened in helpless misery until their eyes became heavy. Soon they slept the sleep of exhaustion, only to jerk into guilty denial when he suddenly appeared, obviously (and untypically) plaintive about their being asleep. Three times that scene of helpless exhaustion, denial, guilt, disappointment, was acted out. Finally the sequence ended by the added horror of the sound of marching feet, the blazing torches blinding their eyes, the shouts, the violence, the unbelievable sight of the soldiers surrounding him, the final obscenity of Judas' kiss.

Suddenly guilt and frustration broke over them, and Peter, as always, was the catalyst. With an oath which had probably drifted across the lakeside a hundred times, he pulled a sword and lashed at the official nearest to him. The man fell clutching his head. Jesus moved from those holding him, who let go as if mesmerized, and gently tended the man's wound until the screaming stopped, the breathing steadied, and he stood up again. Then the three of them lost control and ran madly among the trees, sobbing and panting until the night fell silent around them and they stopped, hearts pounding, eyes stung with tears. All this they remembered long after. We can only guess how they thought of it or spoke of it. Perhaps it was difficult to speak of it at all. We certainly wish to eradicate the memory of agony, and sometimes we succeed at the conscious level. But they performed one service worth all the mistakes, all the guilt, all the self-reproach. However ineffective they were, the important thing is that they were there.

Perhaps when he asked them to come with him into the garden, Jesus wanted nothing more than that they should be with him. At that particular time it would seem, from his subsequent intense disappointment at finding them asleep, that their support meant everything. Sometimes there are occasions in our dealings with the agony of others when all we can do is to be there, to be with them. There are occasions when no words need be said, no solutions offered, no encouragement given — maybe for the terrible reason that there is no solution possible. At such times we often hide our own fear, perhaps stifle a desire to run from the situation (how plentiful are the excuses which come to mind!). We may feel inarticulate, clumsy, inadequate — and indeed, maybe we are! But the gift demanded is not articulation, competence, or wisdom. Love demands only that we be its mediator, merely by being present.

The Decision Makers

That same day Herod and Pilate became friends; till then there had been a standing feud between them.

Luke 23:12

Only a few yards away from the Via Dolorosa in Jerusalem, pilgrims may purchase crosses. These are made of various materials — some crafted in silver and bearing a precious stone in the centre. They evoke many different responses — "lovely," "simply beautiful," "how much," and "I'll take this one." The cross with accompanying chain ("that will be a little extra") is wrapped in tissue paper and placed in a suitable box.

Such purchases may reflect anything from casual acquisition to deep devotion. If the latter, this small, glittering cross centred on its shimmering, milky stone can open windows on a terrible reality. Suddenly, with two-thousand years torn away, the cross springs to life-size. It is no longer metal and gem; it is two separate wooden beams. One, already planted firmly in the dry, brown earth, is standing and waiting a mile outside the city. The other, a huge, roughly-shaped crosspiece about seven feet long, is biting into the skin of a prisoner's shoulder as he drags it through the street leading to the city gate. When he falls, it crashes down beside him. With an efficiency born of long experience, the Roman officer seizes an onlooker from nearby and orders him to take up the fallen beam. By that chance incident a north African visitor is forever registered in history. Bearing the cross, Simon of Cyrene staggers out from under the welcome shadows of the gate and up the slope of the hill.

None of us ever shares the cross by choice. We are, by nature, onlookers to agony. It both fascinates and repels us because we know that, if it is not ours now, it soon will be. Time and circumstance call us out of the crowd to take up the cross, and we do so only because we have no choice.

We must remember that Simon most likely felt no particular religious devotion. He did not see himself enshrined in the script of a divine and eternal drama. He was not aware of bearing something defined in religious language as "the cross of Christ." He knew only that he had had the bad luck to be standing precisely where the prisoner stumbled. Likewise we, when the "bad luck" of cross-carrying comes, in pain or illness or sorrow, find it difficult to understand that we are sharing in a universal suffering, the long-ago agony of Mary's Son, the eternal pain felt in the heart of a God who himself suffers for a fallen universe.

What is true of Simon is true of every actor in the drama of our Lord's Passion. We who witness it through the lens of history ascribe immense stature and significance to the actors. We discover and imagine and analyse all kinds of complex motivations in the decisions of Pilate, the betrayal of Judas, and the manipulations of Caiaphas. Yet we have to remind ourselves that none of them saw themselves through such a lens.

For Judas the experience probably added one more chapter to his many failures to give himself completely to anybody or anything. That realization may have swept over him in a great tide of sadness which deepened to despair and finally to suicide. For Caiaphas those days of frenzied lobbying simply maintained a routine dedicated to preserving the fragile civil order. For Pilate, leaving the city for his pleasant coastal villa in Caesarea, the incident may have strengthened the link with a devious and dangerous Herod, before whose great wealth, judiciously invested in the Roman connection, Pilate himself was so vulnerable. Perhaps too he felt the sour taste of another compromise made, another test passed in the degrading process of political survival in an impossible administrative post.

Whatever it meant to Judas, who would have undergone a searing personal agony, the betrayal and execution of Jesus came to Caiaphas and Pilate as a problem in administration, one of the unpleasant but inescapable decisions of their "nine to five" lives, a decision which afforded no perfect resolution, and therefore called for executive action.

None of these men saw themselves or their actions in some universal, moral, or religious context. Their betrayals and guilts and self-diminishments were the same as ours, carried out in the ongoing tasks of their daily lives. We would do well to study these three very carefully, not as figures of condemnation, but as reflections of our own ambiguities and guilts.

The Messenger

Mary of Magdala went to the disciples with her news:
"I have seen the Lord!" she said, and gave them his
message.

John 20:18

In the weeks after his resurrection there were many encounters between the disciples and their Master. What is very important to notice is that in every such encounter Jesus points them to tasks they must do as a community. Even when the encounter is with an individual, as with Mary of Magdala near the garden tomb, she is discouraged from treasuring the moment for herself. The conversation turns very quickly from her joy. Instead she is pointed away from the encounter itself. She is to go and tell the community. The supreme irony of the story is the quality of the community she was sent to. It was abysmal!

As Mary moved away from the garden, beside herself with conflicting emotions, wanting both to stay with him but wanting also to tell the unbelievable news to others, we know only too well what the situation was elsewhere. Somewhere in the city, probably west of the temple area, and almost certainly within the vision of the Roman sentries patrolling the Antonine Tower, there was a group of traumatized men crowded into a single room, standing or sitting or lying in various stages of nervous exhaustion from restlessness to deep sleep. They had lived through a week-end of unbearable intensity culminating in a horror they had been warned repeatedly to expect but had found impossible to conceive until it took place. It was to this paralyzed group that Mary was sent from the encounter in the Garden.

What paralyzes our capacity to act? Usually we feel that the situation is too much for us. The task of recovery is too complex, too threatening, too demanding. There are Upper Rooms all over Western Christianity. The sounds of contemporary civilization jar our senses and immobilize our powers. The old simple and comfortable institutional Christ has been taken by events and crucified on the cross of a cold, secularized, and harsh society. For many there is little to do but gather dutifully and sing the ancient songs in a strange and hostile land.

Yet into the terrified silence of that long ago room comes the sound of running feet up the outside steps, the ecstatic knocking at the door, the gasping figure tumbling in among them, the strangled message. After a moment's paralysis one man leaps for the door, and a moment later another follows, and the door swings shut again, leaving Mary to collect her jangled nerves.

Where are the feet hurrying to the nervously closed doors of today's church? Where is Mary of today's Magdala? In the group of young people annoyingly asking for new songs? In the mistrusted couple who asked to begin a Bible class? In the person trying to share the experience of healing and laying on of hands? With what a frantic spectrum of reaction they are received, just as she was so long ago. Yet in every congregation there are some who will move toward the news which is pushing the locked door open, some who have unlocked the doors within and outside themselves, and who will seek the unlocked tomb of the Good News. Then once again Life himself will be abroad in the city!

It is important to see this passionate and courageous woman running, not just through ancient Jerusalem, but running in a thousand disguises through today's city, toward today's scattered Christian communities. All too often, when an individual today discovers that the reality of Christ demands serious and conscious allegiance, or discovers in a way totally beyond words and analysis and description that Christ is, for him or for her, truly alive, then that person may dismiss the Christian community as irrelevant, as unable to understand the new reality they have discovered. But if they come to the community in all its seeming ordinariness, they will discover two or three who will move with them to check out their discovery. Immediately then the community is affected. Something new begins. Christ has died; Christ is risen!

The Visitor

*They were still unconvinced, still wondering, for it
seemed too good to be true. So he asked them,
"Have you anything here to eat?"*

Luke 24:41

During the terrible week-end of Jesus' death and his resurrection
as Lord we have no detailed description of what the disciples
did. We know that they gathered in some house in the city. That
house may have seen a great deal of coming and going — someone
slipping out for groceries, someone anxious to let family know
that they were safe — all the reasons which would be present in
any group in any age hiding out until some danger passes.

At some moment during those hours, probably in the early
hours of Sunday, the group became aware of a new presence
among them. It is quite pointless for us to argue and analyze
how that came to be. Till time ends we will wonder about it, and
we will choose whether to dismiss it as legend or believe it as
faith. Luke describes it with absolute simplicity. He says, "As
they were talking about all this, there he was, standing among
them" (Luke 24:36). It's a timeless sentence about Christian
experience. Time and time again Christians and their churches
enter periods of agonized self appraisal and self criticism. What
has gone wrong? Why has this aspect of Christian life become
weak or decadent? What should we do? What should we change?
Should we have conferences? To do all this is perfectly human
and in no sense being sneered at. But what is essential to realize
is that while we are "talking about all this" Christ is "standing
among" us. Somewhere, in some activity, in some group, in
some utterance, in some insight, in some guise he is among us.
He stands not only in that long ago room, on the edge of that
nerve-wracked and exhausted group, but also among all the
wrestlings and efforts of today's Christian experience.

Luke says that they thought they were seeing a ghost. They
thought that, he says, because they were terrified. Today among
some Christians a kind of terror arises from the way they see
their own situation. For them the modern world is a room which
has succeeded in locking out almost completely the elements of
Christ, the elements such as the sense of his presence, faith in

his church, the relevance of Christian theology. Only a pitiable ghost of Christ manages to filter into the locked room of the contemporary world, a ghost who flits around the edge of contemporary experience, who offers vague images and ideas to the apparent realities of sociology, sexuality, politics, and the many other disciplines of our time.

In the face of their terror Jesus avoids explanation. He invites them to touch him. He asks for some food. Nothing is more obvious in defining our humanity than the whole cycle of our digestive processes. To this Jesus turns to communicate his utter reality. As many Christians agonize about their feeling of the ghostliness of contemporary Christianity — its apparent fragility, its distance from most modern issues, its seeming unreality — they grasp for what can give Christ more substance for them.

Notice what Christ himself did in that room to give substance to his presence, what he did more than once in the resurrection appearances. He shared a meal. Nothing speaks more clearly of the substance and reality of faith and community than to share together both the symbolic meal of bread and wine, and the actual meal of friendship, family, or congregational life. The action is filled with earthy, timeless, totally human reality. By communicating the visibilities it points to the invisibilities. The visible bread points to the grace of God; the visible community points to the community of faith in past and future.

Long ago in that room our Lord chose the symbolic meal to communicate the reality of his risen life. Today there is an instinctive turning toward the action of the Eucharist to do precisely the same thing, to communicate the reality in his risen life among Christians today. Luke tells us that a moment after Jesus had eaten with the disciples he began to ''open their minds to understand the scriptures.'' Here is the rhythm of devotional life which is richest for a Christian community. Here also are the problematical polarities of Christian emphasis and loyalty. We call them sacrament and scripture. Here in this simple room, among followers trembling in a fearful ecstasy, our Lord offers both sacrament and scripture as the twin roads towards experiencing his and our and the church's resurrection.

Thomas

He said, "Unless I see the mark... unless I put my finger into the place... I will not believe it."

John 20:25

Thomas is very much a late twentieth-century man. He is pitched between a great longing to believe and a chronic inability to believe. We know that Thomas wasn't there when the unbelievable happened. John tells us a few other things about him. Thomas was always blunt. A spade was called no more and no less.

In the last few weeks of his ministry Jesus was hounded out of the Jerusalem area. He and the disciples had gone north of the city for refuge when a message came that Lazarus was ill in Bethany. Jesus decided to go back, but the rest were very edgy. To go back was really risking everything. Thomas brought the discussion to an end. One can almost hear his dejection when John reports him as saying, "Let us go also, that we may die with him" (John 11:16). The next time that we get some insight into Thomas is in the Upper Room itself. Jesus has just said, "And if I go and prepare a place for you, I shall come again" (John 14:3), and Thomas raspily interjects, "Lord, we do not know where you are going, so how can we know the way?"

So there is a disciple who is not easily impressed by language and concepts, however lovely. Thomas is a bit of a pragmatist. He likes facts. When he arrived among the disciples and was told of Jesus being among them, he responded in typical fashion. "Unless I see the mark of the nails on his hands, unless I put my finger into the place where the nails were, and my hand into his side, I will not believe it" (John 20:25). The tone is blunt but is far from unfeeling. Actually it expresses the determination of a man whose heart has been broken, and who will not easily allow himself to become vulnerable again.

We all long for proof. This age is full of proofs of the divine. Von Daniken argues that God is really a fleet of intergalactic visitors. Huge industries suggest that God is really perfect health. To many God is the earth itself, and concern, love, and care for it is our ultimate service. Among Christians there is a deep longing that the faith be proved true. In recent years the full resources of modern science are being utilized to examine the Shroud of Turin to find if it is really the shroud in which our Lord's body was wrapped for burial. In certain Christian circles there is a thirst for the miraculous, whether it be in spiritual changes or physical healings. "Unless I see," said Thomas, I will not believe."

There could be a hundred reasons why Thomas is not with the others when Jesus first visits them after the resurrection. But when Jesus appears again among them, Thomas is there. Jesus readily offers himself to Thomas in the terms which Thomas understands. And when his doubts have been satisfied, Thomas makes the exclamation of total allegiance, "My Lord and my God." This incident says much to us about the individual Christian and the Christian community.

We live in an age when we long for new resurrection in every aspect of our personal being. We long for it in society and in the church. Though the need for personal religion is always there, and though personal religion has become rich and deep for many again, often in the presence of the community we gain strength, grace, courage, and insight today. This is apparent in the forming of countless prayer and study and Bible groups, the recovery in many places of a communal style of doing the liturgy. From these elements in today's church, millions are able to touch a reality which they did not experience before. In the company of others there is being found a sense of solidarity and a new level of reality. The Jesus Christ known merely as an idea has instead become a reality of flesh and blood shared with other people, seen in the eyes of others, spoken by the lips of others.

Many years later when John was writing the first of his great letters which we have now in the New Testament, he began with the statement, "It was there from the beginning; we have heard it; we have seen it with our own eyes; we looked upon it, and felt it with our own hands" (I John 1:1). As the elderly John wrote these words, he may well have been remembering a time many years before when his old friend Thomas had stretched out his hand and touched the body of their risen Lord.

The Stranger

Two of them on their way to... Emmaus... and they
were talking together... Jesus himself came up and
walked along with them; but something kept them from
seeing who it was.

Luke 24:13

The Upper Room in Jerusalem is of course not the only place
where they were given experiences of his risen presence. Years
later, in a letter to the Christians in Corinth, Paul makes a list of
all the appearances, and he mentions some which are not in the
gospel record (1 Corinthians 15). Among these are a number
which seem almost to intercept the disciples as they begin to
move back into their former modes of life, toward remembered
simplicity.

We are a couple of miles south of Jerusalem. For those who
have been aware that there has been an execution everything is
now tidily put away. The Galilean trouble spot has been eradi-
cated, and political stability has been restored. Pilate, that most
vulnerable of political figures, is relieved that things went as
well as they did. In Caiaphas' house there is an even greater relief
that the menace of Roman punitive action has once again been
postponed. For those to whom the prisoner was more than a
curiosity, the world has ended. The dream of a kingdom, albeit
barely comprehended but nevertheless sown in their hearts in
haunting and gentle images, has been smashed beyond recovery.
Now there remains little to do but to gather together the rem-
nants of their former rural existence and begin to reconstruct
their lives.

Thanks to Luke we know what takes place on this winding
hilly road. We know of the stranger who immediately senses
and describes their mood. We know how he understands their
reference to the disappointment of all their hopes. To their
amazement he weaves their recent experience into the long
tradition which they had learned in childhood. Finally we know
how a gesture made at the table in an inn hits them like a bolt of
lightning and sends them breathlessly back to the city.

Perhaps this episode on the road to Emmaus can speak to us in
our situation. For many Christians in the Western world a certain

90

dream has ended, a dream in which the Christian religion and the Christian church, Christian traditions, thought-forms, and assumptions, carried authority in personal and public life. For some there is disappointment at the ending of that dream.

This feeling creates certain responses. One response is that of a Christian retreat from involvement with the city — the whole realm of political and public institutions. There is a temptation to head for the village — the personal part of life, the family, the home, the suburban. The two who long ago slipped out of the city gate and headed for their village are an eternal image of this temptation.

But, as the stranger met them and revealed to them who he was, so he appears to us on this twentieth-century road. In his timeless way he teaches us again that we cannot opt out of the city, however complex and ambiguous its affairs may be. To strengthen us for those tasks which he brings us back to face, he offers the bread, which is grace in at least two ways. Because it is broken and shared in community, we are reminded that we do not serve him alone, in a parish, office, store, school, university, or social agency. That is his first way of nourishing us. The second is more difficult. He announces the simple but devastating fact that a dream of a certain way of thinking of him is ended. Certain ways of worshipping him, certain ways of presenting his claims to society — these have ended. But the dream and the hope and the destiny which is eternally in his possession and of his creation — this has not ended. And our vocation has not ended. We do not have the luxury of returning to former simplicities, real or imagined.

Luke says of the two travellers that "without a moment's delay they set out and returned to Jerusalem," and that when they arrived "the Eleven and the rest of the company had assembled." When we force ourselves from the nostalgic search for imagined simplicities and return to the seemingly harsh complexities of the present, we find to our surprise that we are not alone. A company had assembled. There is a Christian community waiting to support our resolve and to be enriched by our gifts. Eventually there comes a moment in that fellowship when we are aware, as they became aware, that Jesus is standing among us.

The Ultimate

I have come that men may have life,
and may have it in all its fullness.

John 10:10

Human experience is aware that all the wealth of living — all
the growth, discovery, passion, and beauty which life offers —
must end in death. But our experience is also aware of other,
ongoing kinds of death. Although we can envisage perfect states
of human relationship, social justice, or inner peace, all our
efforts to reach into such a kingdom end in defeat. The best we
can expect is to be given moments in our growing and working
lives, in our loving, in our efforts to be people of integrity and
creativity, when we taste fleeting glimpses of the unity, peace,
or ecstasy we long for.

We witness many kinds of dying. We see the noblest deeds
and the loveliest personalities brutally crushed by others, by
tragedy, or by seemingly meaningless events. We see great
human creations — empires, civilizations, political institutions
— wither and crumble because of some flaw or weakness which
everyone sees but no one can prevent. The name for all this is
today neither fashionable nor frequently acknowledged. In the
Bible it is called "sin." We have made that word into something
petty, and we have forgotten its dark and terrible majesty.

But lest we be overwhelmed unawares by that ominous
power, we seek for something to lift and inspire the human
spirit. In our searching we discover, and appropriate as "the
armour of God," the birth, life, death, and resurrection of Jesus
Christ.

Once in time the ultimate personification of all human beauty,
goodness, and truth offered himself to the total experience of
being born, living, suffering, and dying — as all of us are doing.
He embraced the loveliness of human relationships, the zest for
life, the simple pleasures which make life precious. He also
accepted all the darkness of human experience. He underwent
the thousand deaths we know when love is rebuffed by hate,
truth brutalized by falsehood, integrity mocked by deceit. All
this Jesus embraced, until he gave up the Spirit and the ultimate
perfection of humanity, the mediator to us of the divine nature,

92

entered the mystery which all of us enter and which we call death.

This event human eyes witnessed and human hands carried out in human history. Our ambivalent humanity both wept to see it and also mocked at its agony. But after it was over we became witnesses to another and even greater mystery. The death of Ultimate Man (Jesus) came at the hands of sinful man (you and me), but the Ultimate Man in Jesus Christ continues to live for each one of us today. We know that the ultimate elements in him — love, truth, hope — cannot be destroyed. He rises. As in time and history, all things once rose in Jesus Christ, so they continue to rise in human affairs until the end of time.

Hope, crucified in all of us by despair, rises.
Reconciliation, crucified in all of us by alienation, rises.
Love, crucified in all of us by hatred, rises.
Truth, crucified in all of us by lies, rises.

This is the Christian song which climaxes all the songs of human experience. Its words are "Jesus Christ is Risen." Its music will bring hope to humanity until the end of time. That end, which is beyond our imagining, will itself become a new beginning through the risen power of him who, in the words of St John the Divine, "makes all things new, and is the beginning and the end."

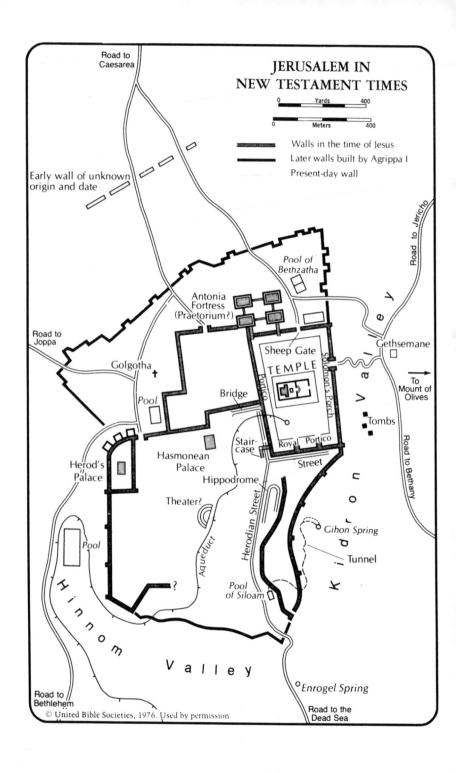

JERUSALEM IN NEW TEMENT TIMES

JERUSALEM IN NEW TESTAMENT TIMES

Road to Caesarea

Yards 0 400

Meters 0 400

Walls in the time of Jesus

Later walls built by Agrippa I

Present-day wall

Early wall of unknown origin and date

Road to Jericho

Pool of Bethzatha

Antonia Fortress (Praetorium?)

Road to Joppa

Sheep Gate

Gethsemane

Golgotha

TEMPLE

Solomon's Porch

To Mount of Olives

Pool

Portico

Bridge

Tombs

Stair-case

Royal Portico

Hasmonean Palace

Street

Herod's Palace

Hippodrome

Theater?

Herodian Street

Gihon Spring

Tunnel

Pool

Aqueduct

?

Pool of Siloam

Kidron Valley

Hinnom Valley

Enrogel Spring

Road to Bethlehem

Road to the Dead Sea

© United Bible Societies, 1976. Used by permission.

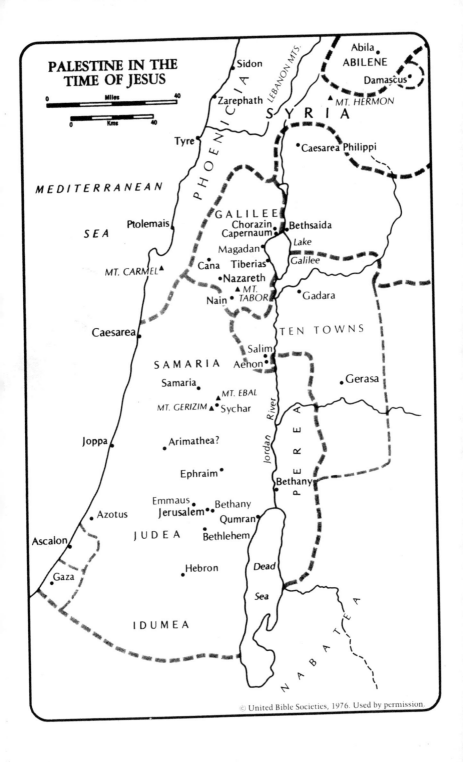

PALESTINE IN THE TIME OF JESUS

Miles
0   40

Kms
0   40

MEDITERRANEAN

SEA

PHOENICIA

SYRIA

LEBANON MTS.

Sidon

Abila

ABILENE

Damascus

Zarephath

▲ *MT. HERMON*

Tyre

• Caesarea Philippi

Ptolemais

GALILEE

Chorazin

Capernaum

• Bethsaida

Lake

Magadan

Cana   Tiberias

Galilee

• Nazareth

▲ *MT. TABOR*

Nain

• Gadara

MT. CARMEL ▲

Caesarea

TEN TOWNS

Salim

SAMARIA

Aenon

• Gerasa

Samaria

▲ *MT. EBAL*

MT. GERIZIM ▲ Sychar

Joppa

Arimathea?

Jordan River

P
E
R
E
A

Ephraim

Bethany

Emmaus

Bethany

Azotus

Jerusalem

Qumran

Ascalon

J U D E A

Bethlehem

Gaza

Hebron

Dead

Sea

IDUMEA

N
A
B
A
T
E
A

© United Bible Societies, 1976. Used by permission.